LEGAL LITERACY

OPEL (OPEN PATHS TO ENRICHED LEARNING)

Series Editor: Connor Houlihan

Open Paths to Enriched Learning (OPEL) reflects the continued commitment of Athabasca University to removing barriers—including the cost of course materials—that restrict access to university-level study. The OPEL series offers introductory texts on a broad array of topics, written especially with undergraduate students in mind. Although the books in the series are designed for course use, they also afford lifelong learners an opportunity to enrich their own knowledge. Like all AU Press publications, OPEL course texts are available for free download at www.aupress.ca, as well as for purchase in both print and digital formats.

SERIES TITLES

Open Data Structures: An Introduction
    Pat Morin

Mind, Body, World: Foundations of Cognitive Science
    Michael R.W. Dawson

Legal Literacy: An Introduction to Legal Studies
    Archie Zariski

LEGAL LITERACY

An Introduction to Legal Studies

ARCHIE ZARISKI

AU PRESS

Published by AU Press, Athabasca University
1200, 10011 – 109 Street, Edmonton, AB T5J 3S8

ISBN 978-1-927356-44-9 (print)   978-1-927356-45-6 (PDF)   978-1-927356-46-3 (epub)
doi: 10.15215/aupress/9781927356449.01

Cover illustration: ©2014 Phil Bliss c/o theispot.com
Interior design by Sergiy Kozakov
Printed and bound in Canada by Marquis Book Printers

Library and Archives Canada Cataloguing in Publication
Zariski, Archie M., 1949-, author
      Legal literacy : an introduction to legal studies / Archie Zariski.

(Open paths to enriched learning (OPEL) series, 2291-2606 ; . 3)
Includes bibliographical references.
Issued in print and electronic formats.

      1. Law--Canada--Textbooks. 2. Sociological jurisprudence--Canada--Textbooks.
I. Title.

KE444.Z37 2014   349.71   C2014-901205-5
KF385.ZA2Z37 2014   C2014-901206-3

We acknowledge the financial support of the Government of Canada through
the Canada Book Fund (CFB) for our publishing activities.

Canadian   Patrimoine
Heritage   canadien

Assistance provided by the Government of Alberta, Alberta Multimedia
Development Fund.

Government

This book is dedicated to Kim, with love.

CONTENTS

PREFACE

The inspiration for this text is partly autobiographical in nature—it reflects issues I have confronted in my life. My first career was as a lawyer practising in the field of litigation, where I became fluent in the discourse of legal argument at trials and appeals. The evidentiary techniques, legal jargon, and adversarial strategizing I learned at law school were put to good use in the service of clients large and small. After fifteen years of this work, the thrill of battle wore off and I became interested in more cooperative ways to solve legal problems. I had also always wanted to teach. Consequently, I resolved to become a law teacher, with the aim of training lawyers to be problem-solvers instead of gladiators.

My next career was launched when I obtained a graduate degree by researching the then-new field of alternative dispute resolution. As a novice teacher, I came to see that traditional law school pedagogical techniques often reinforced a confrontational mindset among fledgling lawyers, encouraging them to view themselves as privileged insiders in the legal system without much concern for the real needs of their clients beyond winning the court battle. Lawyers were being trained from day one to see society exclusively through "legal eyes" that keenly recognized legal concepts and issues arising in everyday events, but were blind to clients' underlying desires and the emotions that motivated them. Many call this "learning to think like a lawyer." It could also, I think, be considered a dehumanizing educational process that should be changed.

Early in my teaching career, I came into contact with students in legal studies who were eager to learn about the law, but not necessarily for the purpose of becoming a lawyer. They needed some of the same knowledge and technical capabilities employed by law students, but were less tolerant of jargon and traditional law school pedagogy. I decided to start teaching some law subjects, such as research and writing, to both legal studies and law students in a more accessible and less elitist way.

As a teacher of alternative dispute resolution (ADR), I became aware of the wider field of socio-legal studies, where it was born and nurtured. Scholars of anthropology, sociology, psychology, and other disciplines have looked at law and legal processes as a subset of other individual and social phenomena. Their studies have illuminated the connection (and disjuncture) between law and society. ADR scholars have focused on the particular ways in which legal systems respond, or fail to respond to social conflict, and critics, such as those in the access to justice movement, and have asked questions about whom the law really serves. Increasingly, these and other perspectives on law and how it is practised have made their way into law schools.

As a student of the economic analysis of law, I learned that the material conditions of law practice and legal processes can have real effects on outcomes for clients and society as a whole. Some of the traditional elements of our legal system, such as legal publishing and information dissemination, seemed to be impediments to a fair justice system. The barrier of copyright and prevalence of legal writing that is unclear and full of jargon can be at least partly blamed for the widespread ignorance among the population of their legal rights and obligations. Once again, I decided to adjust my teaching practice in order to bring it in line with the requirements of plain language and equitable access to legal information.

Most recently I have become engaged with the open access movement in law and education. As a faculty member of an open university that offers distance education, I have a keen appreciation for the public's need for quality education and sound legal help. This experience has led me to value legal literacy, not as an indicator of the professional superiority of lawyers, but as an essential capacity for all citizens in a society permeated by law. And thus I have written this book, dedicated to educating all about their legal rights and objectives, and to improving law through informed critique, and articulating the demands of the society it serves. I believe everyone should know how law seeks to achieve justice in and for society, not for law's sake alone.

I acknowledge and thank anonymous reviewers of the manuscript who pointed out shortcomings and suggested improvements. Thanks also to Pamela Holway and Connor Houlihan, editors at Athabasca University Press, for their insight and encouragement which stimulated completion of the book; Elaine

Fabbro at Athabasca University Library for exploring the world of online legal research with me; and students in the legal literacy course at the university who continue to pose fresh questions about law and legal systems.

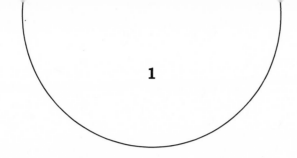

1

INTRODUCTION

This book is for readers who wish to know enough about law and legal systems to be able to accomplish something within the law or to go about changing it. In other words, the information found here should help readers accomplish some legal tasks themselves and offer a constructive critique of law and its institutions. "Legal studies" is a term with a broad meaning but is usually contrasted with "law studies" or "studying law," which are most often used to describe preparation for professional practice as a lawyer. Studying law is comparable to learning a new language. Students in law schools report feeling that they are being taught to take on a new identity as part of learning to "think and speak like a lawyer." As a result of intensive immersion in legal culture during the course of their studies, lawyers emerge with a distinct view of the world and a specific language to express that vision. They largely lose the ability to both think and speak as anything other than a lawyer. Legal studies, however, attempts to preserve what we might call students' "bilingual" or "bicultural" capacities by allowing them to see the world simultaneously like a lawyer and a layperson.

It is the critical aspect of legal studies that helps students preserve an "external" view of law and the legal system. Although lawyers accept some responsibility for criticizing and improving the law, most of their efforts are directed at assisting clients to achieve their goals within the existing legal system. Lawyers and judges take a mostly "internal" perspective on law as professional "insiders." The student of legal studies should instead demonstrate an ability to take both an internal and external perspective on the system.

Legal studies takes an external perspective on law similar to that found in the "law and society" and "socio-legal" approaches to research and scholarship.

From such perspectives, law and society interact (though not always on equal terms), each continually reshaping the other. Socio-legal studies, as part of the social sciences, aims to find enduring concepts, models, and theories about the intertwining of law and society and only incidentally concerns itself with the actual reform of legal institutions. By contrast, the critical wing of the law and society movement was initially focused on how law could be used to transform society, making it more egalitarian and inclusive. The focus in this book, however, is more on how members of society may transform law from the inside out using the tools of the legal system. A critical external perspective on law may reveal the need for legal change, but an internal perspective and traditional legal methods may be necessary to achieve some improvements.

Canadian examples are mostly used in this volume, but the general principles, concepts, and ideas presented are relevant to all legal systems that draw on the British legal tradition: the United Kingdom itself, Australia, New Zealand, other Commonwealth nations, and to a lesser extent, the United States. Such systems belong to the "common law" family of legal traditions and institutions, in which the decisions of judges in individual legal cases brought to trial establish the law by setting precedents that will be applied in later, similar disputes. Thus, law is built "from the ground up" as it were, with decisions in particular disputes becoming accepted as the basis for law commonly applied throughout the nation. Law is also created in common law systems by legislators in parliaments and other similar bodies. In common law legal systems, disputes that result in court proceedings ("litigation") thus have a prominent role; this fact has affected many aspects of our legal institutions and procedures.

Over hundreds of years, the process of litigation in common law legal systems has developed characteristics with far-reaching implications for how law is administered and justice is achieved. As a result, common law litigation today incorporates the following characteristics:

1. Justice lies in following proper legal procedures—thus, "procedural justice" is the principal goal;
2. These procedures require debate and discourage dialogue, promoting an adversarial approach to dispute resolution over a cooperative one; and
3. The outcome of these procedures is often unpredictable, although the goal of law is to bring more certainty to human relations.

In other words, justice is the uncertain result of structured confrontation. If you are not a lawyer, you may find this statement about the legal system surprising, perhaps even shocking. If you are a lawyer, you will likely agree and say "yes, law is based on procedural justice and adversarialism, which leads to indeterminate outcomes." From a legal studies perspective, these aspects of our legal system call for an explanation, and perhaps also require reform.

This description of litigation in Canada's legal system highlights the need for those seeking justice through law to be prepared to take an active part in reaching their goal. Legal literacy is the term used in this book to describe the knowledge, skills, and abilities needed to pursue litigation in Canada and other similar common law legal systems. For instance, a person pursuing a legal claim has the responsibility to help prove the facts and make arguments as their contribution to the production of justice. It will therefore be useful for them to know how law and the legal system are structured (the topics of Chapters 3 and 4), and how legal process and procedures work (Chapter 5). Knowing how to find the written materials that comprise the body of law, and how to read them with understanding will also be necessary to pursue litigation (Chapters 6, 7, and 8). The ability to express legal ideas and arguments in a persuasive way to a decision-maker is the final skill this book will explore (Chapter 9). In this book, I will discuss the techniques learned as a part of legal literacy as the "tools" that must be used to fashion justice through law in our legal system. At the same time, from a critical legal studies perspective, I raise questions about the complexity, efficiency, and effectiveness of our present system of litigation.[1]

PROCEDURAL JUSTICE

"Procedural justice" is a term used by psychologists to describe the positive experience reported by people who feel they have been treated fairly while participating in legal proceedings. Feelings of being respected, listened to, and understood by legal authorities usually lead participants to be satisfied with the experience, even though the ultimate result may not be what they hoped for. In other words, people who feel they have been treated fairly consider the process they have gone through to be "just," although they might question the justness of the outcome. Procedural justice can be compared to "substantive justice," a term describing a result that is correct according to a universal standard of justice and is therefore acknowledged to be just by everyone concerned.

Modern Western nations such as the United Kingdom, Canada, and the United States are heterogeneous societies with significant numbers of immigrants who have contributed a wide variety of cultures, religions, and philosophies to the mix of beliefs, ideas, and attitudes we observe around us today. In such societies, universally accepted standards of justice have little chance of taking root. Law is not thought to embody divine will, and judges are not considered to be divinely inspired. These circumstances make it difficult indeed for legal institutions in Canada and similar countries to achieve substantive justice. There will always be some who disagree with a ruling.

From a legal studies perspective, this represents a serious imperfection in our legal system because it could lead to disrespect for legal institutions and law in general—the problem of maintaining the legitimacy of the legal system in the eyes of the public. Legal systems faced with problems of legitimacy have focused on procedural justice as the answer to public doubts about their capacity to deliver substantive justice, and this has been an effective response.

Here are some examples to give a better understanding of the concept of procedural justice. Section 7 of the Canadian Charter of Rights and Freedoms (included in Canada's Constitution) reads in part:

Legal Rights

Life, liberty and security of person

7. Everyone has the right to life, liberty and security of the person and the right not to be deprived thereof except in accordance with the principles of fundamental justice.[2]

Reading this, you might think that the phrase "in accordance with the principles of fundamental justice" means something like "in accordance with a set of rules (or a code)" that determines the just result in any dispute about individual rights. But that is not what it means to lawyers and judges. For them, these are the minimum required procedures to follow in order to arrive at a just result. The Supreme Court of Canada noted in a recent case considering the meaning of Section 7 to be that "fundamental justice" simply requires a law not be arbitrary, that its adverse effect on people is not disproportionate to any public benefit, and that it does not do more than is necessary to accomplish its purpose.[3] Provided these criteria are met, governments may pass any law they consider desirable, and it cannot then be challenged in the courts under Section 7. These are essentially procedural restrictions on making law—provided legislation is written carefully, with these guidelines in mind, governments may legally limit everyone's life, liberty, and security.

Here is a second example of procedural justice in relation to decision-making that leads to action by government authorities. It is now well accepted in the law that such decisions must be made according to principles of natural justice and fairness. Again, the Supreme Court of Canada has confirmed what this standard means. In a recent case, the court established that even when collecting a debt, governments are bound by the duty to use procedural fairness, which involves giving notice to the debtors and receiving responses from them.[4] These procedural steps constitute justice in that situation, but in the end they do not relieve a person from paying what is due.

Finally, here is an example of the importance of procedural justice in criminal law. The Supreme Court of Canada has confirmed that a procedural irregularity during a criminal trial that is an error of law may amount to a substantial wrong or miscarriage of justice, and can lead to a conviction being thrown out.[5] Such is the strength of the law's concern for proper procedure.

Procedural justice is a response to the reality that people in our society do not agree on universal standards of justice which lead to the absolutely correct result in every situation. Instead, we accept a legal system that delivers justice according to the law by following a series of legally approved steps, or "legal procedure." If these procedures ensure fair treatment of the people involved, we believe procedural justice has been provided, and we accept the results. In other words, the process of following the correct procedures produces justice. Thus, justice is the result of well-planned action, not something already present that merely needs to be revealed. This description of justice may be hard to accept if you are not a lawyer, but it is familiar if you are, because legal education includes learning to take the right steps at the right time—that is, lawyers become experts in legal procedure. What procedural justice means for someone pursuing their legal rights is that they must become actively involved in producing justice for themselves, and cannot just expect someone else to discover and accept the justness of their claim.

Procedural justice requires that the procedures to be followed are well designed to accomplish their purpose. A common design of the litigation procedure is to find out what has happened (the facts) by commenting on the situation (the argument) to persuade the judge to use the appropriate rules (the law) in order to reach a rational decision (the judgment) that does justice to the parties.

I will examine and critique the litigation processes and procedures found in Canada and similar legal systems in detail in Chapter 5.

THE ADVERSARIAL SYSTEM AND ADVERSARIALISM IN LAW

A second distinct characteristic of common law legal systems is their reliance on the adversary system to propel and manage litigation. The adversary system requires parties in dispute to take primary responsibility for pursuing their claims (or maintaining their defences) by collecting evidence and presenting it to a judge, along with their arguments, for decision (adjudication). In other words, the court is not expected to become actively involved in preparing a case for trial. The role of the judge is merely to hear what is presented by each side, and then to decide which party has put forward the best evidence concerning the facts, and the most persuasive arguments about the law. The adversarial approach to litigation stands in contrast to the inquisitorial approach found in most legal systems that are not based on British common law traditions. In an inquisitorial system of litigation, the judge takes primary responsibility for collecting evidence and preparing a case for decision, although the disputing parties also contribute to the process.

In the common law system, the expectation that the parties will pursue the dispute themselves without significant intervention by judges or other officials continues throughout all steps of the legal process, including the trial, where disputants present their evidence and arguments in whatever way they see fit, constrained only by the rules governing how trials are conducted. Courts refuse to "second-guess" the parties, and thus judges decline to intervene in deciding how cases should be presented, calling this a type of "paternalism" inconsistent with the adversarial system.[6] Everyone is required to follow proper legal procedures and to pursue their claim diligently and independently, whether or not they have the assistance of a lawyer. This is made clear, for example, by Rule 1.1 (2) of the Rules of Court of Alberta, which states, "These rules also govern all persons who come to the Court for resolution of a claim, whether the person is a self-represented litigant or is represented by a lawyer." Judges will offer some extra guidance to parties without lawyers, but an impartial decision-maker must avoid becoming an ally. Chief Justice McLachlin of the Supreme Court of Canada put it this way, "The trial judge may try to assist, but this raises the possibility that the judge may be seen as 'helping,' or partial to, one of the parties."[7]

The adversarial approach to justice makes a person with a legal claim responsible for finding their own way through the legal system with minimal official assistance. Lawyers are available to help, but many cannot afford them. This form of litigation is consistent with Western modes of thought that emphasize polarity and dichotomy (for example: true/false, good/evil, right/wrong). A trial judge who hears two versions of the facts must choose which is to be believed as true, and which of two legal arguments will be accepted as right and correct. Adjudication in common law systems therefore consists of declaring a winner and a loser based upon the strength of the cases researched, organized, and presented by the parties. Litigation uses the methods of confrontation and debate as the primary means of resolving disputes. In doing so, it follows Western traditions of scientific inquiry, in which a hypothesis and its negation ("null hypothesis") are tested by searching for data that tend to confirm one idea or the other. The Western practice of political decision-making based on debate is also reflected in adversarial legal traditions. Scientific knowledge and democratic politics are examples of the value of confrontation and competition in discovering the secrets of nature and choosing wise courses of action, and these models lend support to the value of the adversarial system in law. Legal studies, however, continues to question whether human affairs are best understood in the same way as nature, or whether wisdom is always as simple as deciding right from wrong.

Adversarialism is the term used to describe the attitudes and practices of disputing parties in such a system of litigation. Some of the attitudes connected with adversarialism are competitiveness, secretiveness, and distrust. Adversarial practices include manipulation, stalling, evasion, and sometimes deception, encouraging confrontation and discouraging cooperation between disputing parties. Lord Denning, a famous English judge, once remarked, "In litigation as in war. If one side makes a mistake, the other can take advantage of it. No holds are barred."[8] In another case, Denning noted that "as a matter of justice, a party must prove his case without any help from the other side."[9] Thus, the parties to a legal dispute are expected to engage in vigorous "partisan advocacy" for their competing positions[10], which discourages cooperation through dialogue as an alternative way of arriving at a just result.

Procedural justice based on adversarialism encourages combativeness and contradiction, behaviours that have been criticized as unnecessary and ineffective in achieving justice. Many have promoted "therapeutic" and "problem-solving" methods as more humane and creative ways of resolving disputes within the existing legal system, but the adversarial approach continues to be dominant. The alternative dispute resolution movement I describe in Chapter 4 encourages cooperation and dialogue outside the constraints of legal processes and procedures as a better path to justice. Critical legal studies questions whether the results obtained through the adversarial system of litigation are sufficiently beneficial to excuse the behavioural excesses often associated with it.

The following examples illustrate the adversarial system in practice. In criminal matters, a report of harm is followed by a police investigation, which may result in charges being laid in the name of the state against an individual (the accused) who is alleged to have committed the crime. The state and the accused person are clearly adversaries with opposing objectives: legal authorities wish to see a criminal punished, and the accused wishes to avoid punishment. Non-criminal legal matters arise through a process of "naming, blaming, and claiming"[11]: a person recognizes they have been harmed ("naming"), identifies another person as the cause ("blaming"), and asks that person to rectify the situation ("claiming"). When the identified person refuses to act as requested, a dispute comes into existence.

If law is used as a reason for making or refusing a claim, we call it a legal dispute, whether or not legal proceedings are commenced. This process is straightforward if you claim that someone has failed to repay a debt they owe you, but less clear when you claim that their failure to be careful triggered a chain of events that resulted in your injury (called "negligence" in law). Whatever way the claim arises, in non-criminal legal disputes (known as "civil" cases), the person claiming and the person claimed against are also considered adversaries. Important consequences result from considering opposing sides as adversaries in legal proceedings, most notably the climate of adversarialism that envelops (and some would say poisons) litigation.

UNCERTAINTY AND INDETERMINACY IN LAW

Law is expected to bring order and predictability to society by requiring people to act in specific, lawful ways, and prohibiting them from acting outside of the defined norms (unlawfully). We expect others to obey their duties under the law, and they in turn expect us to respect their rights. Order in human relations is thus maintained by laws that strike a balance between our freedom of action and others' freedom from interference. The certainty of law also allows us to predict the consequences of our actions. When we know the limits of lawful behaviour in advance, we can avoid becoming involved in legal disputes.

Recently, however, the certainty of law has been called into question. It is now increasingly difficult to be confident in our knowledge of what actions are lawful or not, and we do not know what the decision will be if they are called into question through litigation. The outcome of adjudication is described as increasingly indeterminate—instead of a single, predictable result, only a range of possible decisions can be foreseen, some supporting one disputing party, and some the other side. This results in uncertainty for all members of society, who find it more difficult to predict the legal consequences of their actions. Uncertainty and indeterminacy in law can generate doubt about the value and legitimacy of our legal system today—another issue that may be explored in critical legal studies.

Indeterminacy in litigation may occur in every step of the legal process: finding the facts; selecting and understanding the law; and making a rational decision that is both consistent with similar cases and also achieves justice between the particular parties. This changeability is surprising because law is usually regarded as a contributor to increased certainty in human affairs by warning and encouraging everyone to act lawfully, thereby making social life more predictable. When going about our daily business, most people operate in what has been called the "shadow of the law," and expect others to do likewise. Such a beneficial effect may well occur most of the time, but when a concrete legal dispute erupts, the certainty of the law is called into question through adversarial competition by the parties involved. A dispute encourages opposing sides to shine a spotlight on the law, and to disagree about its shape and shadow. This process highlights the importance of interpretation of the law during legal proceedings, which I will consider in Chapter 8. Rarely will any law be so clear that no conflicting interpretations are possible.

Not only may the law be called into question in the course of a legal dispute but also the facts of the case. Adversarial procedures encourage a disputing party to challenge the accuracy and truthfulness of the evidence presented to support the opposing side's case (we will examine evidence in legal proceedings further in Chapter 9). In many cases, opposing parties present conflicting evidence, thus requiring a judge to consider which side has provided the most convincing version of the events in question. The judge's "finding of fact" (the decision about what the evidence proves) often depends on careful comparisons of many different pieces of evidence, or making conclusions about the credibility (believability) of witnesses, and the results are often unpredictable.

As we will see in Chapter 4, the principle of precedent in the law is used to achieve consistency in decision-making over time and between different courts and judges. Its basic idea consists of resolving similar disputes in a similar way. Precedent therefore contributes to predictability in common law legal systems, where new law may be generated in individual cases. In theory, if one party presents a precedent (a past decision made in a similar case) to a judge, one can predict with relative confidence that the judge will follow the precedent and reach the same decision.

The adversarial system, however, encourages the other party to take a contrary position regarding precedent, along with every other aspect of the opposing side's case. One method of calling a precedent into question is to argue that the previous case is not sufficiently similar to the present one, which has its own unique aspects and thus requires a different result. Such an argument is called "distinguishing" the prior case from the current one, with the result, if accepted by the judge, that it need not be followed as a precedent. When one side makes such arguments, a judge faces another difficult task: deciding which prior decisions are precedents that should be followed, and which are distinguishable and so may be disregarded. Because the law does not provide much guidance for judges when making these decisions, the result of an argument about precedent may go either way.

One concrete example of some of the kinds of legal uncertainty I discussed above can be found in a recent case decided in the Court of Queen's Bench of Alberta.[12] As described in the facts of the reported case, there was a collision between two vehicles in the middle of an intersection with no signs or lights regulating the traffic. One car (we will refer to it as the car on the left) hit another coming from its right (the car on the right). The driver of the car on the left argued the accident happened because the driver of the car on the right was speeding excessively, otherwise he would have seen him sooner. At the trial, the driver of the car on the left admitted that he did not see the other vehicle before the collision, but said he was certain it was speeding. There were several people in the car on the right, and all testified (gave evidence orally in court) that the driver was staying at or below the speed limit. The judge concluded that the "weight" (strength) of the evidence was on the side of the driver on the right, and found as a fact that he was not speeding. Both sides in this dispute recognized that a particular traffic rule should be used in deciding the case. It read, "When two vehicles approach or enter an intersection from different highways at approximately the same time, the person driving the vehicle to the left shall yield the right of way to the vehicle on the right."[13]

The driver on the left may have planned to argue that this rule only applies to situations in which both drivers are obeying the law, but not if one was speeding. However, because of the judge's decision about speed, it was no longer useful to argue about how the rule should be understood. The driver on the left also found some previous cases in which judges decided a driver was partly to blame if they realized there would be a collision and didn't take action to avoid it. He urged the judge to follow these cases as precedents and decide that he was not the only one at fault. However, after carefully reading the cases, the judge concluded that the facts in these cases were sufficiently different to not be considered precedents. Finally, the driver on the left argued that the medical evidence presented about the other party's injuries showed he did not take his doctors' advice and therefore should have made a quicker recovery, thus reducing the amount of compensation he was entitled to. The judge disagreed. She concluded the other driver made reasonable progress in his medical treatments, and awarded him the compensation he requested.

This case is a good example of some of the indeterminacy encountered during litigation in an adversarial legal system. Although drivers do not usually plan their trips with arguments about the law and legal precedents in mind, when they are involved in a collision they may understandably expect to be able to determine quickly and with certainty which party is legally liable and thus responsible for the damage. With such knowledge, a dispute can be settled by agreement, thus avoiding the time and expense involved in prolonged litigation. This is one reason why we may question the functionality of a legal system that necessitates adjudication, involving great uncertainty over the probable result, to resolve such disputes.

THE TOOLS OF LEGAL LITERACY

The preceding sections have described some of the challenges facing those who seek justice through litigation in an adversarial system:

- the correct process must be chosen and required procedures followed;
- the parties involved must make progress without much official help;
- each side in the dispute will oppose and compete with the other all the way; and
- there is usually no guarantee of success, despite an individual's best efforts.

At this point, the reader may well conclude that common law litigation is a minefield which should only be approached under the guidance of a lawyer. The legal profession would support that view, since it serves its own interests. Today, however, the cost for legal services of all kinds, not just representation in litigation, is too high for everyone except larger businesses and the rich. The result is that many individuals and smaller organizations must either litigate without lawyers, or else abandon their legal claims. The proportion of self-represented parties (called *pro se* litigants in the United States) is growing in both Canadian courts and those of similarly developed Western countries. The causes of and possible solutions for lawyers' high fees can be explored from both critical legal studies and economic perspectives, but that subject is beyond the scope of this book. What I will examine is the potential for legal literacy to address some of the unmet needs for help that have been created by the unaffordability of professional legal services. Legal systems in Canada and elsewhere face a crisis of legitimacy, if access to the courts is practically non-existent due to lawyers' fees. The price of justice is now simply too high. One solution to lawyers' effective monopoly over the production of justice through litigation may be extending legal literacy more widely in society.

Legal literacy provides techniques (called tools in this book) to meet the challenges of litigation without a lawyer. As I discuss in Chapter 2, these tools are taught to lawyers, but they may also be learned by non-lawyers who wish to gain a critical understanding of law and to work toward justice within the legal system. The key tools for effective action in an adversarial legal system are:

1. Legal analysis: using legal concepts and ideas to identify and describe issues (the decisions a judge will be asked to make about the facts and the law) that arise in specific situations. This analysis informs the choice of the appropriate legal process to follow to resolve those issues. Legal analysis also acts like a filter to separate legally relevant actions and events from irrelevant matters which may be disregarded when applying the law.

2. Legal planning: charting a course that involves taking the proper steps at the right times to facilitate adjudication of the legal issues raised. Procedural steps in law are designed to be fair to both sides of a dispute, but adversarialism encourages parties to try to use them for their own advantage. Good planning should include all the necessary steps, including those to be taken at trial.

3. Legal research: discovering support for the arguments to be made concerning the issues that have been identified, including those arguments critical of the other side's case. Legal analysis is only the starting point for understanding and action in law—the initial legal analysis will be expanded and deepened as more facts and perhaps more issues are uncovered. Finding precedents is one goal of legal research, and another is discovering interpretations of law that strengthen arguments about how the law applies to the facts.

4. Legal communication: communicating in a credible and effective way, both orally and in writing, about the claims that have been made and the issues to be decided. Legal arguments take a variety of particular forms that must be mastered and responded to when made by the other side.

The term "legal capability" has recently been used in the United Kingdom to describe the knowledge, skills, and attitudes people require when faced with legal issues.[14] A report put together by the Public Legal Education Network investigating legal capability developed a diagram to identify the skills and abilities required at various points in response to a legal problem (Figure 1.1).[15] It clearly shows that the concept of legal capability is similar to that of legal literacy used in this book.

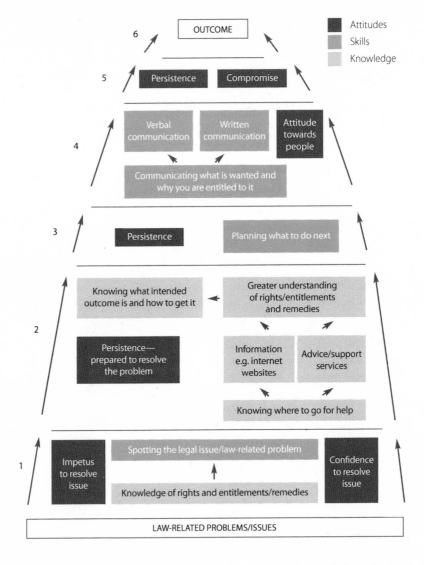

Figure 1.1 Diagram illustrating the skills and abilities needed to work through a legal issue. Courtesy of the Public Legal Education Network.

In Figure 1.1, the tool of "legal analysis" is described as "spotting the legal issue" based upon some prior knowledge of law and legal rights. "Legal research" is included in the step of getting help from advisors and information sources such as the Internet. "Planning" is shown as the third step toward resolution, and "communicating one's claims" along with the arguments that justify them is the final step toward the desired outcome.

In this volume, the tool of legal analysis will be the focus of Chapters 3 and 4, while I address legal planning by discussing legal processes and procedures in Chapter 5. The sometimes peculiar language of law can be an obstacle to legal analysis, planning, and research, so I explain it in Chapter 6, while I discuss methods and techniques of research for legal purposes in Chapter 7. Law does not speak for itself; it needs to be interpreted, a part of legal argument. Chapter 8 is devoted to some of the principles of interpreting legal materials. Finally, in Chapter 9, I give some guidance about communicating effectively to advance legal goals.

CRITICAL LEGAL LITERACY

Legal concepts and their complex, meaningful relations form one of the foundational structures of law, as I will discuss in Chapter 3. These building blocks are produced through processes that are legal (such as statutory interpretation), political (for example, litigation over voting rights), and economic (for instance, using litigation with competitors as marketing by other means). The tools of interpretation (see Chapter 8) and legal argument (discussed in Chapter 9) may be used to rework legal concepts that need to change. Such concepts may be those like "necessity," "fairness," and "the reasonable man," where the legal meanings no longer reflect common understandings in society.

One of the messages of this book is that the law, its concepts, and ideas may be improved by critique and also by using the tools of legal literacy to bring about progressive change within existing legal systems. As figure 1.1 shows, engaging with the legal system requires strong personal motivation, persistence, and hope. When joined with knowledge, planning, and effective communication, it's possible to achieve good results that also benefit others.

For instance, Lucie E. White wrote about guiding a poor, devout black woman, the sole parent of several young children (referred to in the case as "Mrs. G.") through a hearing to decide if she should lose her social assistance benefits because of an overpayment.[16] One way the penalty could be avoided according to the law was if the money she received was spent on "necessities." As part of her evidence, Mrs. G. revealed that a good part of the overpayment was spent on new shoes for the children to wear to church ("Sunday shoes"). This was unplanned testimony, and did not become a factor in the ultimate decision. However, it might have been used by the lawyer as part of an argument that the word "necessities" should be interpreted with regard to all of the particular circumstances of Mrs. G.'s life, and not limited to a standard bureaucratic definition of what is "necessary." Such an argument might not succeed, but it would be a respectable attempt to secure justice for Mrs. G. using legal tools. White concludes her reflections by expressing respect for the "activities that poor Black single women with children—citizens—undertake for themselves, on their own ground" which may change the law and society.[17]

The redefinition of marriage to include same-sex unions in a number of countries is a recent example of individuals successfully remaking law from the inside. Lawyers and their clients made convincing legal and political arguments to persuade courts and legislators to enlarge the definition of marriage beyond the union of heterosexual couples.

This book is intended to help the reader understand the tools that people use to produce justice, and how to use those tools themselves when they are pursuing the necessities of their own lives through law. In the concluding sections of each chapter, I will explore some possibilities for change in law and society which add a critical perspective to the knowledge of how the tools of legal literacy function. The next chapter considers what legal literacy means in more detail, and compares it to other forms of literacy that are important in our society.

CHAPTER REVIEW

After reading this chapter you should be able to:

- explain what is meant by the term "procedural justice"
- describe the adversarial system of law and explain the term "adversarialism"

- discuss the concepts of uncertainty and indeterminacy as they apply to law
- list the principal skills and techniques that comprise the "tools" of legal literacy
- explain what is meant by the term "critical legal literacy"

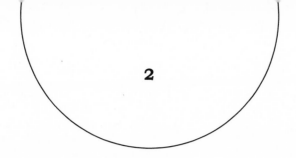

2

LEGAL LITERACY AND OTHER LITERACIES

Examining the Concept and Objectives of Legal Literacy

In this chapter we will examine in more detail the idea of literacy in law both in a functional and critical sense. Literacy today means more than just being able to read—it encompasses understanding society so that one is able to function within it, and be capable of working to change it for the better. Legal literacy in this expanded sense thus involves knowing the constraints and possibilities law offers for change, plus having the capability to use its tools and techniques to improve society for oneself and others.

LITERACY AND LAW

To become literate (able to read and write) is to become a full member of a written language community. If someone is only capable of oral expression, they are not a full member of the community that uses the written word. Being able to write extends the range of a person's words far beyond hearing distance; being able to read vastly increases the number of other people whose words can be experienced. Being literate is considered such an important capacity that the United Nations has labelled it a human right. Literacy has also been described as essential to healthy families.

Being literate can therefore be seen as a crucial way in which an individual connects and interacts with society around them. As the South American educator and social activist Paulo Freire puts it, "reading the word and learning how to write the word so one can later read it are preceded by learning how to write the world, that is, having the experience of changing the world and touching the world."[1] Literacy can empower an individual to influence the society around him or her more effectively. The relationship of literacy to law is a strong one, particularly in Western societies with a long tradition of written and published laws.

To the extent that written law helps to form society and guide the actions of its members, literacy becomes important for participation in a legal system. Without literacy, people can become intimidated and alienated from law. This may create a situation where people come into conflict with law, or are unable to obtain help from it. Courts have recognized the barriers raised by a lack of literacy that interfere with asserting guaranteed rights effectively, especially when parties have no lawyer to represent them. In addition, literacy requirements have been used to block access to the political system through voter registration procedures in some jurisdictions, such as the southern states in the U.S. Lack of literacy can disadvantage citizens in many ways.

Organizations at all levels of society are engaged in education to increase literacy levels. However, even basic literacy may not be enough to allow an individual to effectively participate in a legal system.

> Even if people with low literacy have found a way to cope with their daily routine, they find it very difficult to read, understand, and use material related to legal problems. They do not understand the concepts contained in the words, even if they understand the words themselves. Therefore, they cannot understand what is expected of them and often the implications of what is being said.[2]

In modern societies with vast amounts of written law and complex legal systems, it is necessary to go beyond basic literacy in order to understand and use law. Today, the concept of legal literacy has been expanded to include all of the knowledge and skills required to interact effectively with the legal system.

Originally, the term legal literacy was used to refer to an aspect of professional legal education. To be legally literate meant that you, as a lawyer, were capable of reading and writing the legal arguments, briefs, opinions, judgments, and legislation that contribute to the body of law. This definition describes legal literacy as being "literate in the law." In this sense, legal literacy is primarily a concern of legal writing programs in law schools that teach students to think and communicate "like lawyers."

Later, a broader meaning of legal literacy became more common as a result of two different approaches to the concept. One approach considers legal literacy as a capacity spread along a continuum, with lawyers and judges at one end and relatively incapable non-lawyers ("laypersons") at the other. This approach was adopted by the legal scholar James Boyd White, who considered legal literacy to mean "that degree of competence in legal discourse required for meaningful and active life in our increasingly legalistic and litigious culture."[3] Another legal writer describes legal literacy as a "spectrum of functional skills"[4] related to the conduct of litigation. According to the continuum approach, a certain degree of legal literacy is required for effective participation in modern society, but it is not necessary for the average citizen to reach the professional standard that law schools traditionally require.

The second recent approach to the meaning of legal literacy is to consider it as a metaphor. According to this view, the term is "intended to suggest some parallels between the institution of the law, and a system of language to be mastered, knowledge gained and understanding achieved."[5] Legal literacy can thus be compared to learning the language of a foreign society in order to be able to operate effectively within it. For those who lack legal literacy, the world of lawyers and judges feels just as foreign as an unfamiliar country.

The views I have described have led to an expanded conception of legal literacy today that extends beyond the profession of law and into the community. Numerous broad definitions of legal literacy have been advanced. Here are some influential ones:

> Full legal literacy goes beyond the development of a basic legal
> competence and implies the acquisition of knowledge, understanding
> and critical judgment about the substance of law, legal process and

legal resources, enabling and encouraging the *utilization* of capacities in practice.[6]

The ability to make critical judgments about the substance of the law, the legal process, and available legal resources, and to effectively utilize the legal system and articulate strategies to improve it.[7]

The ability to understand words used in a legal context, to draw conclusions from them, and then to use those conclusions to take action.[8]

Legal literacy is a process of self and social empowerment that moves women not only to activate the rights they do have, but to redefine and reshape the inadequate ones as expressed in law and in practice.[9]

Common to these definitions is an emphasis on the ability to take appropriate action in response to problems involving the law. It is understood such action may sometimes be critical of, and challenging to, the legal system. Such a view of what legal literacy means is in keeping with the idea of becoming a member of a community. Membership "has its rewards" as the advertisement says, but it also has its demands. To become the member of a language community is to accept many rules and conventions about how to communicate, but it also entails the ability to challenge those constraints in a way that will be understood and perhaps accepted by other members. So it is with law. Becoming legally literate is gaining full membership in a community that shares a legal system. Such membership comes not only with many constraints but also many opportunities for action and change.

OTHER LITERACIES

In the twentieth century, consumers rose in stature and power as an interest group within society, while the traditional professions came under criticism for being unresponsive and paternalistic. The increasing public availability of information in digital formats has also challenged professional monopolies over expert knowledge. Taken together, these trends have resulted in new approaches to professional practices that are more collaborative in nature. Professionals have begun to involve their clients more actively in decision-making and problem-solving, based on shared information and knowledge. In order to play a more active role in securing their own welfare, laypeople have been encouraged to develop a deeper understanding of professional fields that were formerly considered the domain of experts only.

The development of the modern concept of legal literacy can therefore be seen as part of a movement to empower citizens and to free them from domination by professionals. From this point of view, legal literacy is only one of many capabilities that must be mastered in contemporary society in order to enjoy a free and productive life. Legal literacy alone will not yield all of the benefits of full and active membership in an interconnected and interdependent society, so it is important to understand and embrace other literacies as well. Today, many fields of knowledge and practice have their own equivalents to legal literacy in its expanded sense.

Perhaps the most conspicuous example of another type of literacy today is *information literacy*,* which has grown out of the concept called *computer literacy*. Once computers became readily available in society, there was a movement to educate as many people as possible to understand their functions and uses. As the amount of data available via the Internet increases dramatically, most recognize that the skills of locating, analyzing, and evaluating this information have become crucial for success both in business and private pursuits. Thus the majority of educational institutions today provide students with opportunities to enhance their information literacy. To the extent that the information available online is legal in nature, information literacy shares many of the same goals as legal literacy.

Health literacy is another prominent parallel development to legal literacy. It has been defined as "the ability to access, understand, evaluate and communicate information as a way to promote, maintain and improve health."[10] Public health groups recognize that low health literacy can jeopardize an individual's health in the same way low legal literacy can affect their legal rights. Health literacy includes being able to use some of the same type of tools and techniques as legal literacy, such as searching for and analyzing medical and scientific information in order to make informed choices about future actions.

There are numerous other literacies similar to legal literacy. *Numeracy* is the equivalent in relation to scientific and mathematical understanding.

---

* Words in italic can be found in the glossary.

Financial literacy is considered necessary to manage money and investments. *Environmental literacy* is a knowledgeable appreciation of the limits of our planet to cope with human activity. *Media literacy* involves the capacity to access, utilize, and evaluate communications in various media.

Other literacies share many similarities with legal literacy. They represent ways in which non-experts can acquire the knowledge, information, and capability to act effectively in various spheres of social life without relying entirely on professional help. Like legal literacy, many other literacies also focus on developing a critical appreciation of social forms and practices, and the ability to challenge them when it is thought necessary.

Socio-legal scholars have used other concepts besides literacy to describe the interaction of people and laws, and we will look at some of these next.

RELATED SOCIO-LEGAL CONCEPTS

There are other useful concepts concerning law that may help to put legal literacy in perspective. Three of these are *legal consciousness, legal mobilization,* and *legal socialization. Legal consciousness* is a socio-legal term that refers to awareness of law and legal institutions, together with attitudes toward them, among members of the public. It helps us to understand the significance people attach to the law in relation to their everyday affairs. Legal consciousness can be studied in relation to popular culture, which often portrays law, lawyers, and judges in the entertainment media and helps to shape public ideas and attitudes toward them. Legal consciousness is also related to the concept of norms, which is used to describe everyday expectations of proper behaviour, including etiquette, morals, and laws. Some rules that are usually followed are not law but merely norms, so legal consciousness may not be required in some areas of life.

Studies of legal consciousness show how law helps to frame the perceptions people have of their lives, and to constitute the relations they have with others. Such interaction with the law can take many forms, including avoiding or accepting it: "people make claims on the law, but not necessarily rights claims; the law leads people to accept and acquiesce to existing social and economic arrangements without making them 'lump' their grievances; and people may reject the formal apparatus of the law even as they create viable substitutes for its power and authority."[11]

The concept of legal mobilization refers to how people actively appeal to law and legal institutions to advance personal and group interests. Thus, it is closer to the concept of legal literacy than legal consciousness because mobilization emphasizes the instrumental use of law by those subject to it. It differs from legal literacy in that mobilization usually builds upon existing law rather than offering a critique of it, as legal literacy promises to do. In the past, mobilization meant the processes by which disputes enter the formal legal system, but more recently it has been described as the strategies used by individuals and groups to focus the attention of both legal institutions and the public on their justified grievances. Several scholars have noted that mobilization of law may not yield the intended results because the existing legal system and processes tend to support the *status quo* rather than change. Effective legal mobilization may therefore also require challenging those established legal processes and systems.

Legal socialization is a term used when studying individuals' relationships to the legal order surrounding them. It describes how people internalize, identify with, or reject the law and legal institutions. Some have criticized the application of the concept of socialization to law as an acceptance of law as it is, however oppressive or unjust, and emphasizing conformity to it. Other scholars however, have given legal socialization a more liberal meaning so as to include people's critical perspectives on the law. They believe that the highest level of legal socialization demonstrates a concern for justice rather than just simple obedience to law.

Tapp and Levine take the point of view that legal socialization "works to clarify and elaborate reciprocal role orientations and rights expectations in relation to law, not to institutionalize blind obedience or preach the goodness of specific rules."[12] They go on to define an individual "who lacks the knowledge of rights and resources, the sense of self, and the problem-solving competence sufficient to mobilize the law" as legally impoverished.[13] Legal socialization as a social process encompasses interaction between individuals and the legal system that may lead to mutual change. In this respect, it is a concept that is compatible with, and supportive of, legal literacy.

The concept of legal literacy suggests a number of goals to those who are interested in it. Chief among them are dissemination of information and increase of knowledge about law; empowerment of individuals to make active use of law, and support for constructive criticism of law. These may be described as the educational, competency, and critical goals of legal literacy.

The educational goal of legal literacy has been most prominent, and is often linked to wider programs promoting basic literacy. The idea of public legal education, or community legal education as it is sometimes called, has attracted legal professionals and others interested in promoting legal literacy for many years. Educating people about their legal rights and responsibilities has often been a public service performed *pro bono* (without charge, for the sake of the public's interest) by practising lawyers, and law students have done the same in conjunction with legal clinics attached to law schools. Community and public service agencies have also been active educators for legal literacy, hosting public talks and publishing legal information pamphlets.

Law-related education is the term used to describe education for the promotion of legal literacy among students and is sometimes linked to citizenship education. For young people not in school, "street law" education programs have been created to reach out to youth who are or who may come into conflict with the law. Education for legal literacy has also been targeted to other groups in society considered to be in special need of it, such as teachers, academic administrators, business people, doctors, and nurses.

Even so, information and knowledge are not sufficient to ensure legal literacy when people lack the skills and competencies to interact effectively with the legal system. Accordingly, some legal literacy programs focus on helping members of the public to increase their capacity to mobilize law on their own behalf. Examples of this can be found in developing nations where formal legal protections for women and marginalized groups, for instance, are often not pursued. In such situations, education and training is necessary to increase people's capacity both to understand the law and their competency in asserting the rights to which they are entitled.

Critical legal studies combine legal literacy with a critical perspective. In addition to mobilizing the law for oneself, legal literacy involves working with legal tools and techniques to reshape law and the legal system so that it is more equitable and responsive to everyone's needs. Such work requires an apprecia-tion of the strengths and weaknesses of current legal structures, processes, and procedures. However, encouragement and support for critical perspectives on the law and legal institutions remains the least emphasized objective of legal literacy. Probably this has much to do with the involvement of the legal profes-sion in legal literacy programs. Professionals are more likely to support existing institutions in their field than they are to criticize them. Lawyers, for instance, become accustomed to traditional court practices and procedures, and they are efficient in operating within them. Changing the way they carry on their work involves new learning, adaptation, and will probably be an expense.

Changing the legal system to better accommodate members of the public (particularly self-represented parties), while at the same time inconveniencing lawyers, is therefore never easy and seldom welcomed by the legal profession. Nevertheless, many appreciate the value of informed critical perspectives on the law. For instance, scholars have drawn a connection between levels of legal literacy and economic development that acknowledges the value of criticism for the improvement of legal institutions. Particularly in developing coun-tries, it has been noted that legal institutions which need to modernize and become more responsive to social needs can benefit from increased legal lit-eracy among the public. A society that knows more about its legal rights and responsibilities is less likely to turn to extra-legal or violent means for securing change, and may be more likely to mobilize law with both a critical perspective and reforming objective. Thus, the Asian Development Bank has stated that "dissemination of information regarding legal rights can be the starting point for communities to mobilize on a common platform to achieve legal and policy reforms."[14] This is a recognition that peaceful legal progress can occur if people have sufficient knowledge about law and the competency to engage with it.

The following chapters pursue all of these objectives of legal literacy. In them, I will present information about the law, its systems, and the processes designed to increase the reader's knowledge of these aspects. I will introduce and teach strategies and skills for interacting with the legal system. For these chapters, the goal is to improve the reader's understanding of law and abil-ity to function in legal contexts using the tools of legal literacy. Most import-antly, critical perspectives on each topic will be presented in order to encourage reflection on how the law and its institutions may be improved through critical legal studies.

After reading this chapter you should be able to:

- describe the relationship between literacy and legal literacy
- compare and contrast legal literacy and other literacies
- explain the relationship of legal literacy to other concepts related to law in society
- list the objectives of legal literacy

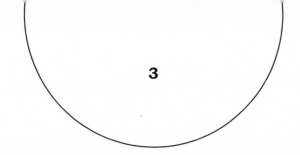

3

LEGAL STRUCTURES

Structures of Law and Legal Institutions

Law attempts to describe and control the social world, just as physics and chemistry describe and manipulate physical reality. The sciences work with concepts such as atoms and molecules, and like them law has concepts that can be used as building blocks to describe and create complex relationships, rights, and obligations. Seeing society through a legal lens—being able to choose the right legal terms to describe people, objects, and events—is a key step in legal analysis, an important tool for justice, and a major component of legal literacy. If you become involved in a situation that is described by someone else in terms of a legal problem, then they have done some legal analysis (correctly or not), and you can build on (or challenge) their analysis. However, if you wish to take the initiative in law, it will be up to you to choose the appropriate legal concepts and ideas to start building your case. The task of legal analysis first requires some understanding of the way law describes the world—its conceptual structure. Law also provides structures for legal action—legal institutions—and we will look at those as well.

CONCEPTUAL STRUCTURE OF LAW

At the foundation of modern Western law is the concept of an actor, recognized as having legal rights and responsibilities. Such an actor is given the status of being a *legal person*; this includes the right to commence legal proceedings, and the obligation to defend him or herself if sued. Things such as trees and animals are not legally recognized persons, although some suggest they should be given legal rights so that proceedings can be taken for their benefit or protection. Children have legal rights and responsibilities, but in most places they are not permitted to take legal proceedings on their own—they must have an adult act for them (sometimes called a *guardian ad litem*). Some important legal persons are the *sovereign* (in the United Kingdom, Australia, Canada, and other constitutional monarchies called the *Crown* or the *Queen*), the *state*, individual human beings, and some organizations such as incorporated companies.

The Queen, as sovereign, is the symbolic source of all legal authority within a geographical area such as Canada. The word "state" can be used to describe this physical territory, but it is also used to mean all of government including its three main structural components, called the branches of government— the *legislative branch* (Parliament, Legislatures), the *executive branch* (Prime Minister, Premiers, Cabinets and public authorities) and the *judicial branch* (judges, courts). The Queen's authority is represented and acted upon by state officials according to law. The state may act in three ways in relation to law. It may make law by passing legislation; invoke the law (for example, when a prosecutor lays a charge against someone accused of a crime); and administer the law (for example, through a judge who presides over a trial).

The most familiar legal person is an adult human being. Although individuals cannot make or administer law acting only on their own authority, they are entitled to call upon the legal system to protect or advance their interests under what is called the *rule of law*. According to this principle, people should be able to make use of law, even if it means challenging actions of the state or its officials. Being recognized as a legal person is therefore an important status— the United Nations has declared it to be a universal right: "Everyone has the right to recognition everywhere as a person before the law."[1]

Because being a person recognized by law is such an important matter, it has resulted in legal disputes and laws being made to govern specific situations. The most notable of such laws are those that include corporations within the meaning of a legal person. In Canada, as a result of legal challenges, it has been determined that the word "everyone" in Section 7 of the Charter of Rights and Freedoms does not include corporations because they are incapable of enjoying rights such as "life, liberty and security of the person."[2] However, it has also been decided by the courts that "everyone" in this section includes all individuals who are physically present in Canada, whether citizens of this country or not. Because the individual is the primary legal actor and bearer of rights in Western law, it is difficult for groups of people (other than corporations) to assert collective rights. For commercial purposes, corporations are given the rights of legal persons so they may enter into contracts and obligations in the same way as individuals.

In addition to legal actors, the concept of *legal rights* is an important part of the foundational structure of the law. Rights may be acquired in two ways: they can be given directly by law—for example, the rights recognized in the Charter mentioned above—or created through voluntary action, such as by entering into a contract that bestows rights to each party. Associated with the concept of rights are the concepts of *legal obligation* or *legal duty*, which require a person to respect others' rights and refrain from interfering with them. Under the rule of law, every legal person should have access to the law to protect or enforce their legally recognized rights.

It is perhaps surprising that the concept of justice is not a foundational one in the conceptual structure of law in the legal systems of the United Kingdom and Canada, although they are both based on the rule of law. Justice is not comprehensively defined in law, but rather is considered to be the outcome of following correct legal processes and procedures. Thus we speak of "justice according to law" without specifying in advance the just result. In Canadian law, we find justice mentioned in the Charter of Rights and Freedoms as "fundamental justice," where it provides the basic standards for lawful action, and in the phrase *natural justice*, which describes the minimum procedural safeguards for a fair hearing. Therefore, it is not a good legal argument to simply state that justice dictates a particular result. A judge's response to such a statement would likely be that justice according to law requires evidence and arguments to be presented. Justice in Western law is the end result of following legal procedures, but not part of the structure of law itself.

As a conceptual structure, modern Western law can be described as totalizing and finalizing. It is totalizing in the sense that it can be applied to any situation, even those that have never occurred before. A recognized legal concept will be found to describe (legally *characterize* or *categorize*) any facts that arise. This is not to say that the law will always intervene in every situation. The result of legal characterization may be a decision that the situation is not something which should be governed by law—in legal terms, it is not *justiciable*. For example, when judges consider an act to be a purely political decision or a matter of foreign policy they will not intervene, and instead declare the matter to be not justiciable.

The law can be described as finalizing because a dispute will never be left undecided, or disposed of simply by the flip of a coin. A decision will be reached, based on law, for every dispute that is brought to trial, although disputes can also be ended without a trial by *settlement* based on the two parties reaching an agreement.

Western law has been structured according to two different conceptual frameworks. Continental European states (and the province of Québec in Canada) have adopted the *civil law* approach, which consists of a complete code of law put in place by legislation. Such bodies of law are called *civil codes*, and all accepted legal concepts can be found within them.

The other way many Western nations structure legal concepts is the *common law* approach, and consists of a mix of statements of law contained in *legislation* (written law passed by elected lawmakers), plus rules and principles of law mentioned by judges when deciding cases. Case decisions—or *judgments* in the common law system—therefore also contain important statements of legal concepts. Legal concepts are stated and collected together in civil law codes while common law concepts are found both in legislation (such as *statutes*) and judgments making them more difficult to survey. In Canada, the common law system prevails, except in Québec, where certain matters are governed by a civil code.

Because it is totalizing in nature, modern Western law contains a large number of legal concepts so as to be applicable to every conceivable situation. Under the common law system, the organization of such concepts is largely arbitrary and based primarily on their relevance to common situations or events. A typical Canadian legal encyclopedia found in a law library is therefore arranged alphabetically by general topic of practical concern. Accordingly, headings mostly use ordinary words and phrases, from "Animals" to "Income Tax" and "Wills." However, under each major heading, unique legal concepts are listed that may not be familiar to the average person. For instance, in an entry for "Contracts," there will be subsections dealing with important concepts in this area of law such as *offer*, *acceptance*, *consideration*, and *assignment*.

Under the heading "Evidence," there will be information about the concepts of *credibility*, *hearsay*, and *privilege*.

The table of contents of a legal encyclopedia also illustrates how concepts in law are linked, from the most basic to more complex and specific ones. Take, for example, the heading "Judicial Notice," a concept concerning matters that do not have to be proved in court by way of evidence. Below that heading will be subsections dealing with more complex variations of that concept, such as *judicial notice of fact*, and *judicial notice of law*. Below that level there will be even more specific concepts, such as *judicial notice of law stated in legislation*. Consider also the basic concept of legal person that I discussed above. Under the heading "Contract," distinctions will be made among the categories of *minor persons*, *intoxicated persons*, and *mentally incompetent persons*.

A *legal digest* is a reference publication that contains information about legal concepts drawn from both legislation and judgments. It is therefore a good source of knowledge about most of the legal concepts used in the common law system of Canada. Such a publication also gives the reader some appreciation of the range of situations in which the law intervenes in life.

How are legal concepts chosen to describe particular situations? What principles guide characterization or categorization as part of legal analysis? This is the question raised by *framing*, the subject of the next section.

FRAMING USING LEGAL CONCEPTS

Legal analysis requires the use of accepted legal concepts, and the distinct words employed (*legal terminology*) when describing situations encountered in life—this is defined as framing an event in legal terms. Taking care to use recognized legal concepts and appropriate terminology should enable an individual to be properly understood and taken seriously by officials in the legal system. Sometimes legal concepts will first be used by others, such as government officials in an official document, or by the opposing side in a dispute, but at other times they must be found and chosen without much assistance. Legal proceedings do provide opportunities to challenge which legal concepts an individual chose previously and to allow changes in some situations.

Legal analysis starts with choosing appropriate concepts to describe a situation (legal characterization), and proceeds by stating a question (or questions) to be decided by applying the law. Such questions are known as *legal issues*. For example: "Did the other party receive a loan (a debt) that they agreed to repay (by contract), but have not done as they promised (a *breach of contract*)?" Stating the issue in this way allows the claimant to present evidence and arguments about these events in support of a request for a legal decision that money is owed, and a court order that it should be repaid. This process of characterizing an event or situation using legal concepts (such as debt, contract, and breach), and stating the legal issues arising from it is known as *framing* a case in law.

Framing provides the conceptual framework for decision-making. The choice of concepts for framing an issue can have both psychological and legal consequences. The way a case is framed can affect the persuasiveness of an argument, and there are often several plausible ways of framing a legal issue. In the end, it is the framing accepted by the judge or other decision-maker that will be used in determining the result of the case. Framing that appeals to the decision-maker's sense of justice or fairness will have a greater chance of being chosen.

Here is an example of the legal analysis of a dispute between a nephew and his uncle. Some time ago, the uncle voluntarily promised to pay tuition fees if his nephew went to college. Now that the time has come, the uncle has failed to pay. The nephew might frame the situation and the legal issue in one way: "My uncle breached (broke) a contract between us to support me through college by failing to pay when the time came." However, the uncle might frame the situation differently: "Informal discussions between family members such as the ones I had with my nephew do not create a *binding* (legally enforceable) contract, and I am not legally required to pay." The uncle might well add another legal issue in his defence: "If there is a contract, then the law requires it to be in writing, and it is therefore *unenforceable* (not enforced by the court) because I never signed anything." Notice how framing the facts and legal issues tends to support the argument of the person who is putting it forward.

Framing a legal issue is an invitation to a decision-maker to characterize a situation or event in a certain way that benefits the party putting it forward. Characterization of the facts, by a judge for instance, may also be called labelling, categorization, or classification, but it is more than just description. Because of the authority given to the decision-maker by law, legal characterization has significant, sometimes violent, real-life consequences—how a judge frames an event results in one side winning a civil case, and sometimes a loss of freedom in criminal cases. Consider the difference it makes to the accused whether a judge characterizes his act as murder or self-defence. Characterization of the facts in one way or another is sometimes the key decision to be made in a case when there is no real dispute about the law; this is another reason why framing legal issues is so important. Framing the issue well is the first step in winning a legal argument.

Even so, framing a problem as a legal issue can lead to a sense that the situation has somehow been distorted. The legal issue may not fully describe the real needs and concerns of the parties involved. For instance, the nephew in the example above might believe that his uncle made a solemn promise which should be kept, but might not think the legal concept of *contract* is quite right to describe the situation. The word contract in everyday language is usually associated with business; however, as a legal concept it is the only one available that describes a mutually binding legal agreement, and so the nephew must use it to frame his claim. The number of available legal concepts is finite, and the conceptual structure of law evolves slowly over time. These are some of the reasons why people often feel their problems fit awkwardly within the conceptual structure of law when they are framed as legal issues.

Framing legal issues has been described as a process of translation or transformation of peoples' needs, interests, and disputes. These descriptions recognize the difference between how people see their problems, and how the law frames and characterizes them. In particular, it has been noted that the law tends to restrict the questions to be decided, while the parties may want to resolve wider issues between them. Mather and Yngvesson note how disputes are narrowed by framing: "*Narrowing* is the process through which established categories for classifying events and relationships are imposed on an event or series of events, defining the subject matter of a dispute in ways which make it amenable to conventional management procedures."[3] The courts enforce narrowing by using the legal concept of *relevance* to exclude evidence and argument that are not logically related to the legal issues as they have been framed.

Lawyers play a major role in framing their clients' problems as legal issues, and how they do this has been studied extensively. Researchers have found that lawyers help to shape the client's "legal self" to fit the issues at hand. This may include convincing the client that his or her emotions should be ignored or suppressed because they are irrelevant to the issues and obstruct rational problem-solving. Or they may overlook or ignore their clients' non-monetary objectives when making claims for personal injury, disregarding the fact that sometimes injured parties also seek to ensure that similar accidents do not affect others. Courts cannot order changes in manufacturing processes, apologies, or forgiveness, so these are never framed as issues by lawyers, although they may be important to their clients. Monetary compensation, known as *damages*, is usually the only *relief* (remedy ordered by the court) available through litigation. The principle of relevance rules out discussion of any other solutions, even if they are of highest importance for the injured person.

Although the conceptual structure of law is slow to change, it can happen. In the Mabo case in Australia[4], and the Delgamuukw case in Canada[5] for the first time courts recognized land rights for Indigenous peoples. A new legal concept, that of *aboriginal title* (called *native title* in Australia), was introduced to the common law. This development in the law, however, only came hundreds of years after colonization and much struggle by Aboriginal people.

Change in law can also involve abandoning legal concepts, such as the one that occurred with the move to "no-fault" divorce. Because the concept of a "marital offence" (for example, adultery or cruelty) was no longer part of divorce law, the concept of "mental cruelty" was also dropped. Lawyers with clients in no-fault divorce proceedings may discourage expressions of emotion that might have formerly been considered useful because they were relevant to the concept of "cruelty" under the old law. Framing the legal issues in an unemotional way may seem insensitive or unfair to clients, but it is helpful to lawyers who are not trained to deal with emotions.

How lawyers are involved in framing issues leads us to consider legal institutions next. Legal concepts do not impose themselves—they are suggested or required by people acting within legal institutions.

INSTITUTIONAL STRUCTURES OF LAW

What is a legal institution? This question has been studied and debated by philosophers of law, sociologists, and others. Sometimes legally recognized relationships and rights are described as legal institutions, such as the "institution of marriage," or the "institution of private property." This way of speaking acknowledges that certain legal relationships have become so enmeshed in the structure of society that they are part of its foundation, like democracy. In this sense, social practices can become "institutionalized" if they are almost universally accepted and followed. We can also think of institutions as similar to traditions, and thus speak of the "institution" of marking a new court year by a ceremonial procession of judges. In this book, however, we will draw on the related word, "institute," to help us in defining legal institutions. An institute is an organization, and therefore a legal institution is considered an organization connected with the law.

There is some vagueness in speaking of institutions "connected with the law." In this book, organizations that are involved with making or administering law or adjudicating disputes over legal issues will be called legal institutions. Another way of putting it is that legal institutions form part of the framework of the state. They are distinct organizations, but they carry out complementary functions prescribed by law. This is the institutional structure of the law we will examine.

A *constitution* serves to create (constitute) the legal institutions of a state among other purposes, such as recognizing basic rights and obligations. Most constitutions establish *legislative* institutions (such as Parliament) to make law, *executive* bodies (such as Cabinet) to administer law, and *judicial* institutions (courts and tribunals) to adjudicate legal disputes. Dividing legal functions between different institutions is known as *separation of powers*, and helps to prevent the accumulation of all legal authority in a single institution or person, such as a dictator. The names of these legal institutions vary from country to country—above we used the word "branches" of government to describe them in functional terms.

As the supreme law of a state, a constitution is expected to be obeyed by members of all legal institutions, including elected leaders. It is the task of judicial institutions to decide disputes over what the constitution and other laws require, even if this means concluding that state officials have acted unlawfully. This is what is known as the principle of the *rule of law*; according to it, nobody is free to ignore the law, especially the constitution.

If we focus on the structure of judicial institutions, we find they are usually organized hierarchically, according to differing levels of authority. Higher courts in a hierarchy can *overrule* (reverse or overturn) the decisions of lower ones. This form of organization recognizes two realities: the possibilities of error and inconsistency among judges. A single court for all people in a state is only feasible in the smallest of states; most have multiple levels of courts and many judges. Judges are human and may make errors. Also, as we will see in Chapter 7, most laws may be interpreted in different ways by different judges.

A hierarchy of courts allows people to *appeal* (ask for correction of error) decisions they think are wrong to a higher authority, and permits higher courts to resolve differences of interpretation among lower courts in the hierarchy. Errors may thus be corrected and consistency ensured.

The court hierarchy in most states resembles a pyramid, with many lower courts at the base, and a single highest court at the top. Some states have several parallel pyramids (hierarchies), with the courts in each hierarchy dealing with a specific type of dispute, such as constitutional law cases, or religious matters. In Canada there are two hierarchical systems of courts—the provincial courts system and the federal system, which share a single court at the top, the Supreme Court of Canada. Note that there are *intermediate courts* that allow for a series of appeals before a decision made at the bottom reaches the highest court. Since many *administrative boards* and *tribunals* make decisions similar to those made by judges (known as *quasi-judicial* decisions), these organizations can be included at the base of the pyramid. The decisions made by these tribunals can be overturned by courts above them in the hierarchy, particularly if the requirements of natural justice have not been followed.

Each level of courts and tribunals is also organized internally in a hierarchical structure. This means there is a chief judge, chair, or president who is given a title that varies according to the institution. Usually the senior judicial official within a court has only additional administrative powers, and no authority to overrule the decisions of fellow judges or tribunal members. In an appeal heard by a *panel* or group of judges (which may include the chief judge), the decision of the court is that of the majority. For this reason, panels of judges or other decision-makers usually consist of an odd number of members to avoid a tie.

There are many courts and tribunals at the bottom of the hierarchy. Choosing the correct court in which to make a claim is part of legal analysis, followed by planning how to proceed there. The correct court for a particular case is the one with *jurisdiction* over (authority to decide) the legal issues involved in it.

JURISDICTION IN LAW

Jurisdiction is the concept used to relate one court to another in a legal system. It allocates cases to designated decision-makers within the overall structure of the judicial institution. Framing a case by legal analysis should include listing relevant facts that may be disputed, clarifying the area of law relevant to the situation, and stating the legal issues to be decided. All of these factors are relevant to the question of which judicial or quasi-judicial body has jurisdiction to hear the case. The next step of legal analysis after framing involves the question of jurisdiction—identifying the correct *forum* (court or other decision-making body) in which to proceed.

As we saw in the previous section, there are usually many courts and tribunals at the bottom of the pyramid of judicial institutions. Jurisdiction defines which body has the authority to consider cases fitting a certain description provided by law (usually legislation). Three criteria are commonly used in setting the jurisdiction of a particular court or tribunal: geography, the subject matter of the dispute or issue, and procedural conditions.

The principle of *territorial sovereignty* (legal authority within a certain area) of states helps explain jurisdiction based on geography. Sovereignty means that events within the geographical boundaries of a state should be free from interference by anyone outside those borders. Thus the courts of one nation-state should not intervene in matters that take place wholly within another. This principle of sovereignty applies internationally between countries, and also internally in *federal states* that have internal geographic divisions, such as provinces in Canada, or states in Australia and America. The courts of a province or state in a federal system have jurisdiction only over disputes with a geographical connection to their territory. The word jurisdiction is sometimes also used to describe the geographical area governed by a particular court system. For instance, Canada has ten provincial jurisdictions, meaning components of a nation with their own internal court structures and hierarchies.

Jurisdiction based on geography is also relevant where a single court has branches in many locations, each serving a defined geographical area. The branch of the court closest to where the disputed events occurred will usually have jurisdiction over the matter.

The second criteria used to describe the jurisdiction of a court or tribunal is the subject matter of the legal issue or dispute. Subject matter refers to those broad categories of law that are found in the legal encyclopaedias or digests (such as criminal law or divorce), and also sometimes refers to the monetary amount claimed in the dispute. The jurisdiction of the lowest court in a hierarchy is usually limited to cases that do not involve large sums of money (in debts or contracts, for instance) or severe penalties (in criminal matters). Some legal issues, such as *defamation* (harming someone's reputation), are not within the jurisdiction of courts at the lowest level. For other legal issues, such as tax and military discipline, special courts may be set up with jurisdiction over those particular subject matters. The broadest way of classifying courts according to their jurisdiction is by dividing them into two types: superior and inferior courts. Superior courts have jurisdiction over all legal disputes except those that have been specifically excluded from their jurisdiction by legislation. For inferior courts the reverse is true: they only have jurisdiction over those legal matters that have specifically been given to them.

Tribunals and boards with "quasi-judicial" decision-making powers generally have the narrowest subject matter jurisdiction, although some may have a wide geographical jurisdiction, such as the Canadian Radio-television and Telecommunications Commission (CRTC). Some boards have a very narrow geographical and subject matter jurisdiction, such as a municipal decision-making institution like the City of Edmonton Subdivision and Development Appeal Board.

Typically, the higher a court is located in the hierarchy, the wider is its jurisdiction. For instance, provincial *appeal courts* have jurisdiction over all matters falling within the geographic and subject matter jurisdiction of all lower courts and provincial tribunals in their province. In Canada, the Supreme Court of Canada at the very top of the national pyramid has jurisdiction over all types of legal disputes wherever they may arise throughout the country. The jurisdictional pyramid is turned on its head compared to the pyramid illustrating the hierarchy of courts. The top is wide, indicating that the highest court has the broadest jurisdiction, while the bottom is pointed, showing that the lowest courts or tribunals have the narrowest jurisdiction in terms of geography, subject matter, or both.

The final criterion used to define the jurisdiction of judicial institutions is whether mandatory *procedural steps* have been taken. When starting a legal proceeding, the rules of the court or tribunal that has been chosen indicate what steps must be taken to properly commence and advance a case. If certain procedural rules are not followed, the legal institution may not have jurisdiction to proceed. For instance, the rules of an appeal court or tribunal will specify a time period within which an appeal must be started, usually by filing a document with the court. If that deadline is missed, the court or tribunal may not have jurisdiction to proceed with the appeal unless an extension is requested, the court has the authority to give it, and grants the request.

Today, most courts in Canada and elsewhere have websites for a variety of purposes—many include information and charts or diagrams showing the judicial hierarchy in each geographical area, the names of each level of courts, and their jurisdictions. These are a good reference source when analyzing the question of jurisdiction.

The question of jurisdiction is a crucial one in any legal proceeding. If a judicial body has no jurisdiction over a matter brought before it, then that court or tribunal cannot do anything for (or against) you.

CRITICAL PERSPECTIVES ON STRUCTURE

Physical structures affect our perceptions, institutional structures our actions, and conceptual structures our thoughts. Structure can be comforting in many ways. Thinking of the world in terms of its structure can give us a feeling of order, stability, and predictability. We like to live in solid and reliable dwellings, and we also want our social environment to be stable and predictable. The concept of well-defined roles is part of social structure—we know what to expect, at least in general terms, from a teacher, a doctor, or a preacher. Language itself is a structure that allows us to communicate with the confidence that others will recognize and use mutually accepted grammar and syntax so that we can make sense together. Law is another important way we structure our social world.

Nevertheless, structure can also be confining. Just as a family can outgrow its home, social structures can put limits on leading a full and creative life. Structure can also be oppressive if it obstructs change in response to new conditions or needs. There have been many criticisms of *structuralist* views of society. From a structural perspective the institutions of society work together to maintain a coherent and stable state. This point of view tends to support the *status quo*, where the mere existence of institutions is taken to show that they are well designed and equipped to carry out the role assigned to them. As a result of many critiques of structuralism, our contemporary period is sometimes described as a *post-structuralist* era. Two of the leading critics of structuralism were the French philosophers Michel Foucault and Jacques Derrida. Their critiques give us another perspective on legal structures.

Michel Foucault described how powerful interests in society influence the spread of ideas that become accepted as knowledge by promotion through influential discourse.[6] That knowledge in turn helps to shape laws that accord with the views of those whose voices are most heard. Viewed from this perspective, the development of law is only politics in another form, and the conceptual structures of law reflect the demands of power structures in society. Critical legal studies may help us see how legal structures empower some people in society, and disempower others. Those who are most familiar with legal structures are often in the best position to use law to their advantage. Lawyers in particular are comfortable within legal structures. While politicians may be masters of the structure of power, lawyers are masters of the power of structure.

Jacques Derrida argued that language is both a necessary tool and an unavoidable trap for thought. He juxtaposed structure with "play" so as to emphasize the creative and impermanent aspects of language.[7] The concepts we create rapidly escape our control—our authority is fleeting. As one scholar has put it, he called into question "the law of writing in the writing of law."[8] The phenomenon of *deconstruction* described by Derrida leads us to think of law as an always unfinished project, reaching for but never finally grasping justice. For Derrida, justice can never be defined in words that are eternal and pure. He thus cautions us that we should always be seeking to do justice, but never complacent in thinking we have finally achieved it. The institutions of society are therefore never as stable and reliable as the structuralist perspective assumes. The critiques of Foucault and Derrida warn us not to think of the structures of law as natural, inevitable, or unchangeable. In pursuing critical legal studies, one should always keep in mind that legal structures are made and can be remade by society.

Finally, British sociologist Anthony Giddens suggests that social structures have a dual nature—they have power through repeated use, but they are also useful to individuals who may be empowered through them.[9] His theory of *structuration* is a more hopeful view of social structures. Clinton W. Francis has described Giddens' perspective as "the idea that at the same time actors mobilize structure in practice they reproduce that structure, and at the same time structure empowers practice it constrains that practice."[10]

These critiques lead to the view that power structures law, but also that legal structures have power in themselves. Becoming legally literate in a critical way must include analyzing the structures of law to reveal the powerful interests behind them, and finding a way to use the power of legal structure to secure more just results from law.

After reading this chapter you should be able to:

- give examples of different levels of legal concepts
- describe how legal structures constitute the state
- explain the concept of framing
- describe the institutional structure of courts
- explain the concept of jurisdiction

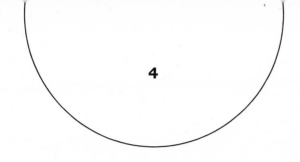

LEGAL SYSTEMS

Legal Systems—Linking Legal Institutions

The dynamic interaction of related structures can be viewed as a system that ties them together for a common purpose. A systems analysis of law includes describing the relationships between and interactions among legal concepts, ideas, and institutions, the operations those institutions conduct, the functions the legal system is expected to carry out, and the observed results. We can thus say that a legal system is expected by society (its "environment") to help maintain peace and stability (its "functions") by producing just decisions ("outputs") in response to legal claims ("inputs"). The term "justice system" is also sometimes used, most commonly in relation to criminal law, as in "justice will be done"—for example, the *Justice System Journal*, which has been published since 1974, focuses in large part on criminal law, procedures, and administration.

Learning how legal systems operate through the work done in interconnected legal institutions should be part of a comprehensive legal analysis in pursuit of justice. If you believe a particular law or legal rule is unfair and want to do something about it, legal analysis will help you find out what type of law it is (where it fits in the structure of law), plus how the law came to be as it is, and who has the power to change it (how the legal system innovates). For example, if the rule or principle has been accepted by the highest court in the legal system, we will see that lower courts cannot adopt a different approach. Legal analysis helps us to understand both the potential for change in legal systems and the constraints on it.

Critical analysis may also discover faults in the legal system, such as systemic biases and discrimination that can affect the justness of outcomes in particular cases and constrains overall system change. Concerning such systemic deficiencies, Susan Silbey asks, "Why do people acquiesce to a legal system that, despite its promises of equal treatment, systematically reproduces inequality?"[1] Perhaps the answer to that question partly lies in the public's general lack of legal literacy skills, including a limited ability to engage in critical analysis of law and its institutions. I noted in a previous chapter that using legal processes to pursue worthy goals does not always result in the intended outcome. When this happens, a critical perspective of legal institutions and the legal system may reveal aspects of them that suppress legal innovation or discourage criticism of prevailing practices. A critical analysis may reveal the need for institutional and systemic change before real progress can be made in using law to improve society. This critical perspective will seldom be heard if most people lack analytical skills in relation to law.

Perhaps the fact that most people are only ever involved in a few (if any) legal cases in their lives also limits the possibility of taking a critical perspective on the legal system as a whole. A person who has lacks experience in a series of legal cases has little basis to make any general observations about the state of the law and its institutions. One of the aims of critical legal studies is to accumulate information and data so that critical analysis may benefit from a broader and longer-term view of the working of the legal system.

A legal system is just one of many systems within a complex society, and can therefore be considered a subsystem of the overall social system. Think of other important systems: health care, education, economic, and political. Historically, many have claimed that the legal system is separate and autonomous from these and other social systems, that it is independent and unique, especially from politics. Although judicial institutions are considered a branch of government, they are expected to operate independently and without influence or direction from the legislative and executive branches. Many now challenge this claim made by courts that they are independent from politics, as we will see later in this chapter, but the legal system continues to draw boundaries between what is considered a "legal" matter and what is not. In this way, the legal system tries to maintain itself as a separate, self-sufficient system with a unique sphere of operation. In the concluding section of this chapter, we will consider how that description should be modified or expanded to provide a more comprehensive view of the legal system as one of many interacting subsystems in society as a whole.

FUNCTIONS OF LEGAL SYSTEMS

Most people, whether they consider themselves to be inside or outside the legal system, would probably agree that one of its main functions is to help establish and maintain social order (not forgetting the contributions of morality, etiquette, and surveillance cameras). But what order means, and how a legal system contributes to it are difficult questions to address, and the answers to them have changed over time.

The most familiar form of law is a set of rules for behaviour: "obey the speed limit," "no smoking," "pay your taxes." Rules help to maintain order and security in everyday life, for example, by making it possible to drive safely on the roads, to live in a healthy environment, and to pay for police who enforce the rules. Law in the form of rules is one method of social control that governs our actions. Under the principle of the rule of law, we expect all members of society, whether politicians, billionaires, or celebrities to obey legal rules—everyone is equally subject to this form of social control.

However, it is important to note that legal systems have very few means of physical coercion over people—the armed forces are not part of the legal system, and not that long ago there were no organized police forces. Outside the courtroom itself, in which order can be forcibly maintained if necessary, a judge relies on the force of her words to exert control over society. In practice, control by legal systems is only possible through society's support of decisions and orders that are considered *legitimate* (legally proper). This principle of *legitimacy* is what impels most people in society to obey the courts, although in a few cases, actual force may be necessary. In criminal matters, control is more obviously exerted by the corrections system following the decisions and directions of the courts.

From time to time, it may become necessary for the legal system to conspicuously reassert control so as to reinforce the rule of law. The most dramatic form of such control is finding someone in *contempt of court*. A person commits contempt when he or she fails to follow the order of a judge and demonstrates lack of respect for the rule of law. Such conduct is considered by the courts to be particularly serious when it is the executive branch of the government flouting the law. When that situation occurs, it challenges the legal system to maintain the force of the rule of law in the face of other sources of power in society. An Alberta case is one contemporary example of how the legal system continues to take such matters very seriously, especially when orders of the court are not obeyed.[2] In that case, the court declared a high-ranking government official to be in contempt of court for not following a court order concerning a child. Contempt can result in serious consequences, such as a fine or imprisonment.

Another function of legal systems is to resolve private disputes between members of society so that people do not "take the law into their own hands" and engage in acts that can escalate into violence. Government, through its judicial institutions, thus offers methods of *dispute resolution* through court proceedings that help to maintain peace and stability in society. Under the rule of law, everyone in society should have access to the courts so that those who refuse to abide by their legal obligations may be summoned to court to answer for their actions and suffer the consequences if found responsible. Most individuals will likely accept adjudicated decisions resolving disputes and comply with them without the use of force if they are made according to accepted legal procedures that are considered legitimate within the legal system. However, if a judicial decision involves payment of money by one *litigant* (party to a lawsuit) to another, it may still be difficult to collect the money owing. In such cases, the property of the *judgment debtor* (party required to pay by court order) may be seized and sold, with the proceeds paid to the *judgment creditor* (party to be paid under court order). Government officials acting with the authority of a court order thus take actions that avert the possibility of confrontation between the litigating parties.

It is now widely recognized that the number of trials in court is declining as a proportion of the number of lawsuits commenced. This seems to indicate that adjudication is becoming a less favoured way of resolving legal disputes. It should be noted, however, that trials as a way of ending disputes have always been exceptional, especially with regard to the great number of potential claims in society that never even become disputes, let alone lawsuits. Most disagreements between people do not become disputes, and most disputes do not become legal claims. The legal system is the last resort for people who cannot obtain what they believe they are entitled to from others, and there are many informal, private dispute resolution methods used in society, such as an intervention by friends or relatives. This might well be the best way of resolving the dispute between the uncle and nephew in the previous chapter. More formal, organized alternative systems such as alternative dispute resolution (ADR) also exist and play a role in the decline in the number of trials; they will be discussed in another section of this chapter.

The dispute resolution function of courts is another way that the legal system indirectly contributes to order in society. Court decisions in specific cases have a *radiating effect*, which means that they can influence others who are not parties to the lawsuit, but who may be in similar circumstances. Knowing the prior decision, others may alter their behaviour with the expectation that doing so will better assert or protect their legal rights. Similarly, people may expect those they deal with to act in accordance with the standards courts have laid down in resolving disputes. This is the spillover effect of individual court decisions; people act in the *shadow of the law* as it has been applied in other cases. In this way, the legal system contributes to establishing and maintaining a set of *normative expectations* (beliefs about what people should do) for society. People tend to act lawfully, and expect others to do likewise based on common knowledge of how the courts would likely treat them in resolving a dispute.

Some legal experts express concern that the decline in trials will weaken the role of the legal system in supporting the normative expectations of society. Those who hold this view argue that trials, as a public display of legal order, are necessary to reinforce the willingness of the public to abide by the law. Some take a different view of the decline in the number of trials. Perhaps courts are finding it difficult to reconcile contemporary developments in society, such as the complex interactions and relationships between people that are facilitated by the Internet, with traditional legal concepts and ideas. Disputants, recognizing such gaps in the legal framework, consequently may take their disputes to other non-legal forums for resolution. Critical legal studies can help us determine whether legal systems are willing and able to embrace appropriate new concepts and develop the normative expectations of a global society.

COURT SYSTEMS

Judges in Western legal systems are expected to be independent, to exercise their own best judgment based on the law and the facts of the case before them.

They are not to take directions about how to decide cases from governments, fellow judges, or anyone else. And yet in the previous chapter, court systems were described as hierarchies, with some judges lower in ranking than others. There is an apparent contradiction in describing judges as being independent, while at the same time subordinate to other judges. Two mechanisms help to reconcile this contradiction: the system of appeals, and the *doctrine* (accepted principle) *of precedent*.

Most legal systems provide for appeals where the decision of a judge in a lower court is reviewed by one or more judges in a higher court. Many legal systems allow for multiple successive appeals from one level of court to another, so that theoretically a decision made in the lowest court may eventually be considered by the highest court in the system. This system of appeals allows higher courts to correct what they believe to be errors made by lower courts. The court that finds an error will usually just substitute a new decision, and that becomes the final judgment in a case. Occasionally the *appellate court* (court hearing the appeal) will order a new trial so that the process begins again.

There is an important limitation in many legal systems regarding the potential errors that may be corrected by way of appeal. The decision of a *trial judge* (or, as we will see in the next chapter, occasionally a jury) includes *findings of fact* (conclusions about what happened) and *findings of law* (conclusions about what the law means and requires to be done). Facts must be proved by *evidence* (information) brought before a judge, such as the *testimony* (statements in court) of witnesses. Usually there is no right to appeal against findings of fact—these conclusions reached by the original judge about what occurred are respected. The trial judge is considered to be in the best position to decide what facts have been proved by the testimony of witnesses and other evidence. In such a system, appeals therefore are limited to questions of law—whether the trial judge made a mistake in interpreting or applying the law.

The appeal system thus helps to reconcile the independence of judges with a hierarchical court system. Appeals allow errors to be corrected after decisions are made; they do not involve giving directions in advance to lower judges to decide cases in a particular way. The independence of judges is thus preserved. But only a small proportion of decisions are actually appealed. How is the hierarchy of courts maintained if judges are free to make decisions that may be wrong, and probably won't be challenged?

The *doctrine of precedent* supplies the other mechanism that maintains hierarchies in court systems. According to it, similar disputes in similar circumstances should be decided in the same way. Most people agree that consistency in decision-making is fair and to be expected from a legal system that is operating properly. Precedent thus serves other functions for society as a whole. When judges follow precedent (make decisions that are consistent with previous ones), they demonstrate that people are being treated equally by the legal system, and are not being discriminated against for irrelevant reasons. If you are in the same legal situation as Jane, you should not be treated differently by a judge just because your name is Joe. Similarly, if you receive a decision from a judge today, it is reasonable to expect that if your case were brought back before the same judge (or a different one in the same court) tomorrow, the result would be the same. These reasonable expectations are supported by the doctrine of precedent.

In hierarchical court systems, the doctrine of precedent requires that judges must decide cases in the same way as higher-ranking judges have decided very similar ones. Because court decisions have been recorded for hundreds of years, it is possible for a court to be guided by a very old judgment if it was made in a similar legal situation. A judge today might theoretically consider a case decided as long ago as the year 1220 as a precedent because the decision in an English case from that year is now available online. With its decisions, the highest court in a legal system thus creates *binding precedents* for all courts below it. For instance, in the case of *R. v. Oakes*, the Supreme Court of Canada established a precedent for the interpretation of the wording of Section 1 of the Charter of Rights and Freedoms.[3] In that case, the Supreme Court set out a series of questions all courts in Canada must answer when deciding the scope of "reasonable" and "justifiable" limits on freedoms protected by the Charter.

The doctrine of precedent thus sets some limits on judicial independence. Judges are not always able to decide cases in the way they think best if there is a binding precedent they must follow. Precedent is justified by the value of predictability it brings to the law. The benefits are well defined by William O. Douglas: "Uniformity and continuity in law are necessary to many activities. If they are not present, the integrity of contracts, wills, conveyances and securities is impaired. And there will be no equal justice under law if a negligence rule is applied in the morning but not in the afternoon."[4] Precedent helps to create the shadow of the law I mentioned above, but indeterminacy makes the edges of that shadow quite fuzzy. Frederick Schauer points out that the doctrine of precedent is based on an exercise of judgment about which cases are sufficiently similar: "No two events are exactly alike. For a decision to be precedent for another decision does not require that the facts of the earlier and the later cases be absolutely identical. Were that required, nothing would be a precedent for anything else."[5] Thus it is not only identical cases that should be decided the same way but also those that are sufficiently similar. This approach opens the way for courts to adapt old decisions to new situations that arise as society changes, but it also calls into question what we mean by "sufficiently similar," thus raising the issue of uncertainty in decision-making that I discussed in Chapter 1. Chapter 9 also pursues the problem of deciding what counts as precedent and what does not when making legal arguments.

When there are significant differences (of fact or of law) between a previous case and the present one, the decision in the earlier matter may be *distinguished* (found to be dissimilar), and thus rejected as a precedent that should be followed. When a judge reasons this way, he or she asserts judicial independence. It is usually easier for a judge to distinguish a previous decision by concluding that the facts rather than the legal issues of the cases are different. Although laws may change, legislation such as the Canadian Charter of Rights and Freedoms rarely does, and therefore a case such as *R. v. Oakes* is likely to remain a binding precedent in Canadian courts for many years to come.

ADMINISTRATIVE SYSTEMS

Government administration is not usually considered part of the legal system, although for many citizens the distinction is blurred. The principle of separation of powers (different functions for different institutions) has been accepted for hundreds of years, according to which judicial functions are allocated to the legal system, and executive functions to the administrative branch of government. Such a division has helped to establish the semi-autonomy of the legal system, so that judges can impose the rule of law on government officials.

Today, however, government administration is involved in a multitude of areas defined by legal rights and obligations, including human rights and discrimination, immigration and refugee claims, unemployment benefits, workers' compensation, and labour relations. Today the wide variety of administrative agencies found within a modern government make many more decisions than courts do that have a direct legal impact on people in their everyday lives. In recognition of this fact, legal systems have adopted a body of rules and principles to guide and supervise administrative agencies known as *administrative law*. Two important operations carried out in government administrations are making *quasi-judicial* decisions (those which impact people's legal rights and obligations) and following procedures that are consistent with *natural justice* (the basic rules of fair procedure). Legal systems ensure that administrative systems make quasi-judicial decisions according to the rules of natural justice through hearing appeals from administrative decisions, or conducting a *judicial review* of administrative decision-making.

Because of their impact on people's legal rights and obligations, we can consider administrative agencies that make quasi-judicial decisions to be part of the legal system. These bodies are sometimes called *tribunals* to differentiate them from courts, although they may also be called *boards*, *commissions* and other names. Administrative systems often operate in a similar way to courts, with appeals from a lower level to a higher one in a hierarchy, possibly with an ultimate appeal to a court. Administrative systems differ from courts, however, in relation to the use of precedent. Precedent is less important in administrative decision-making for several reasons.

First, some administrative agencies are primarily guided by *policy* rather than specific rules set out in legislation. Legislation may give *discretion* (authority to decide what should be done) to officials so they can achieve the best result without strictly following rules laid down in advance. An example of a general policy (expressed as a purpose) which is intended to guide administrative discretion is that provided in Alberta's *Municipal Government Act* in relation to zoning and construction: "The purpose of this Part and the regulations and bylaws under this Part is to provide means whereby plans and related matters may be prepared and adopted . . . without infringing on the rights of individuals for any public interest except to the extent that is necessary for the overall greater public interest."[6] This section identifies an area of administrative regulation where relying on precedent might hinder planners and planning tribunals from achieving the best results with regard to policy changes or perceived changes in the public interest.

Second, administrative agencies do not rely on precedent because they are expected to pay more attention to the unique details of each case than the courts, which categorize cases more broadly. As Frederick Schauer puts it, "some decision-making environments emphasize today the richness and uniqueness of immediate experience. In those environments we seek the freedom to explore every possible argument or fact that might bear on making the best decision for *this* case, for it is precisely the *thisness* of the case that is most vital."[7] In administrative agencies, there is a stronger presumption that each case is unique; therefore past decisions are less helpful as a guide.

For these reasons, administrative systems usually do not follow the doctrine of precedent. However, quasi-judicial decisions achieve a degree of predictability through application of the principle of *consistency*. Administrative decision-makers often consider the value of consistency in dealing with similar cases, although they are not bound by precedent.

Administrative decision-making systems look much like the judicial system when they follow the procedural requirements of natural justice. For example, some tribunals may adopt rules and procedures for evidence similar to those of courts, such as requiring witnesses to swear an *oath* or to make a non-religious *affirmation* having the same effect. Chapter 5 examines the processes and procedures of courts and tribunals.

ALTERNATIVE SYSTEMS

The idea that two or more legal systems might exist within the same territorial jurisdiction is known as *legal pluralism*. Western legal systems have resisted such pluralism because it seems contrary to the principle that every person is equal before the law and that the law applies to everyone. If some members of society are governed by a different legal regime, then they may either unfairly benefit from it or be at a disadvantage compared to others. Further, such pluralism tends to erode the autonomy of a legal system by making its boundaries less certain. Nevertheless, alternative legal systems have existed throughout history and continue to function today. Some examples are the *canon law* followed within the Roman Catholic Church in the Middle Ages alongside national secular laws, and Muslim *Sharia law* that applies today to members of that religion in the otherwise common law country of Malaysia. In some developing African countries, modern legal systems exist together with traditional ones that predate colonization.

From a critical legal studies perspective, we should keep an open mind as to whether legal pluralism may be an appropriate arrangement for certain members of society in some jurisdictions. Another alternative to national legal systems that goes back hundreds of years is *arbitration* (decision-making provided by a person the disputing parties both agree to appoint) for business disputes and religious courts. However, the legal system of the nation-state has often tried to suppress or control these alternative systems by declaring that the decisions they make can be overturned by their courts.

Today, examples of legal pluralism are also found where ethnic or racial communities within states assert rights to their own legal systems. This is usually described as providing *self-government, self-determination,* or autonomy for such groups. In Canada, First Nations have asserted the right to separate legal systems, and there is ongoing debate and discussion about how that goal might be achieved within a sovereign nation-state. Critical legal studies can help us to develop mutual understanding and constructive relations between coexisting legal regimes and positive interactions between indigenous, national, and international legal systems.

Another important alternative today to the dominant national legal system is *alternative dispute resolution* (ADR). ADR was originally viewed as a remedy for the defects in the court systems that made them slow, expensive, and disempowering for the average person. The complexity of law and the adversarial methods employed were criticized for making courts into an ineffective and sometimes inappropriate forum for resolving disputes. Some of the alternatives provided by ADR are *mediation* (negotiation assisted by a third person called a mediator), *conciliation* (where a third person suggests solutions), and hybrid processes such as *med-arb* (mediation followed by arbitration, if necessary). Over the last twenty years, many ADR methods have been adopted by Canadian governments and courts, which have introduced a process called *judicial dispute resolution* (or *judicial settlement conferencing*) that does not involve a full trial.

Alternative dispute resolution processes are now found in almost all Canadian courts and many administrative boards and tribunals. From its beginnings as an "alternative" to formal adjudication, ADR has become part of the mainstream of the legal system in a process of integration known as "institutionalization." Perhaps it is now more accurate to say that ADR is virtually the norm and not an alternative, uncommon way of resolving legal disputes. The widespread availability of ADR today may be one explanation for the decline in the number of trials.

Many ADR processes encourage the disputing parties to craft creative solutions that could not be ordered by the courts and do not reflect strict legal rights and obligations. Although ADR should not result in unlawful agreements, it is accurate to state that settlements through ADR are often indifferent to the law, paying more attention to the commercial or emotional needs of the parties. In some forms of mediation, the legal rights of the parties are debated and weighed in the process of trying to reach a settlement. Nevertheless, a consensual decision reached by the parties in ADR is not a court decision, and does not become precedent for use in future similar disputes. In fact, most ADR processes are private and confidential, so they cast no shadow for the guidance of the rest of society. From a critical legal studies perspective, we might conclude that ADR represents another path to justice that remains an alternative to the path according to law.

State legal systems today face competition from alternative systems of law, and alternative methods of dispute resolution not based on formal law or precedent. The challenges presented by these alternatives are part of the continuing struggle of legal systems to remain relevant and adequate to the needs of the societies they serve.

CRITICAL SYSTEMS ANALYSIS

The phrase legal system, like legal structure, has a reassuring ring to it. It suggests there is a logical, efficient, and effective approach to resolving legal issues in our society. But like the concept of structure I discussed in the previous chapter, the systems approach to law has been criticized. Even if one accepts that a system may be valuable in principle, the way in which it actually functions may still be questioned.

A system can take many forms—from biological (ecosystems), to economic (capitalist or socialist), to digital (artificial intelligence systems). Consequently there are a variety of intellectual influences on systems-based analysis, from evolutionary theory to cybernetics (systems using feedback). All of these related fields have been used to analyze and critique the functioning of law as a social system. Some of the important concepts associated with systems theory are that of the boundary and its associated idea of the external environment beyond the boundary in which the system exists. For a legal system, the environment is the society (which can itself be considered a system) that exists in the territory over which the legal system asserts jurisdiction. If law is intended to serve society, then we can ask questions about how a legal system preserves its boundary while maintaining positive relations with surrounding society. This is one way of examining the tendency of a legal system to consider itself as detached and autonomous within its social environment. As we have seen, there is an advantage to the judicial branch in separating itself from other branches of government, but from a critical perspective we should ask whether such autonomy may also prevent the needs and concerns of society from being recognized and acted upon through law.

Before moving on to other issues, let us look at the question of how to recognize the boundary of a legal system. The problem is much like that posed by the concept of the health system. Should we include health food stores, fitness clubs, and food inspection agencies in the health system? Or is it limited to nurses, doctors (and other practitioners like chiropractors and acupuncturists), and hospitals? Similarly, should we include law schools, building inspectors, and divorce mediators in the legal system?

The traditional approach to defining the boundaries of a legal system revolves around the courts—the more they are removed from them, the less a person, official, or agency is considered part of the system. According to the Alberta government, for instance, the following are participants in the legal system (called the justice system): government ministers of legally related departments; judges, police, lawyers, legal aid, Crown prosecutors, correctional services, non-governmental organizations, victims, and the public.[8] Although people in the last three categories may have contact with the courts, usually it will be brief, and often exceptional. Perhaps the best way of describing a legal system is that it is a network of subsystems (courts, lawyers, police, corrections, government legal offices, and law schools) each with its own dynamics, but all sharing overarching motivations concerning law in society. Viewed in this way, the public is not part of the legal system. So the question is, how do they become participants—how do they cross the boundary?

For those accused of crimes, participation in the legal system is non-voluntary. They are required to attend court and participate in criminal proceedings by police action. People who wish to assert or protect their rights (as *plaintiffs* or suing parties in *civil proceedings* or lawsuits), however, must enter the legal system on their own initiative by commencing a lawsuit. Once a civil lawsuit has been started, the legal system will compel the person being sued (the *defendant*) to respond, or risk having a decision made against him or her if absent. If criminal or civil proceedings are underway, *witnesses* (people with information about the case) may be compelled by the courts to attend a trial and give their testimony. In these senses, the legal system is open to public involvement.

However, the quality of participation by the public in legal processes is another matter. Critics of the legal system have voiced their concerns by questioning whether participation gives the public real *access to justice*. An entire scholarly journal has been devoted to this topic: the *Windsor Yearbook of Access to Justice*. Some of the concerns raised by the movement for increased access to justice include callous treatment of the victims of crime at trial, the stress caused to parties by adversarialism among lawyers, the length and complexity of legal processes and procedures, and the barriers created by legal jargon and terminology. All of these factors make it more difficult for members of the public to use the legal system to their advantage.

As I discuss in Chapter 6, the inability to understand the unique language used in the legal system may prevent members of the public from effective participation in it, and thus impede their access to justice. Further, if assistance is required to make sense of law and follow its procedures, it comes at a cost. The *legal profession* (lawyers) has borne its share of criticism for the high expense of bringing or defending legal proceedings. Governments have responded by providing subsidized services (or *legal aid*), and lawyers by offering free assistance (pro bono) work. However, access to justice for those who are poor has always been problematic, and today even those with average incomes can hardly afford a lawyer. Cultural barriers to participation may also exist for those who have no or little understanding of English or French. Similar concerns about access to justice are echoed in legal jurisdictions throughout the Western world.

A significant feature of some systems is that they act to maintain a stable state of affairs (*homeostasis*) to preserve the smooth functioning of the system. This means that the *status quo* is given priority over change, which can risk destabilizing a system. For social systems such as law, this conservative bias can lead to conflict between the legal system and the society around it. The question thus arises—how does law remain responsive to changes in society?

Several mechanisms can bring about change in the legal system, including passing new legislation that reflects current views in society, promoting *law reform* by agencies formed for that purpose, and through courts being open to new legal concepts such as that of Aboriginal land title. However, it is probable that society will change faster than the legal system. One of the reasons for this slowness to change may be that vested interests prefer current laws that give them valuable rights (think of copyright law), and recalling Foucault, these will shape public discourse against change. Another source that slows change in the law is the weight of habit, ritual, and routine associated with legal processes that has accumulated over hundreds of years. For example, in some common law jurisdictions lawyers are still required to wear horsehair wigs in court, and in Canada, superior court judges are still addressed as "My Lord" and "My Lady," terminology rooted in the feudal past. Finally, as a relatively closed and autonomous system, the legal system is better insulated against change than many other more open and permeable social systems that quickly react to the rapidly changing social, political, and economic environment. A legal precedent may be in development over many years through cases won and lost, but a blog may discuss an idea that topples a government virtually overnight.

A final question relating to the concept of homeostasis is how to define the optimal operating condition of a legal system. How accessible should it be, and how much litigation (civil lawsuits and criminal proceedings) should it process? In the 1970s, many people expressed the view that society (especially in the United States) was too *litigious* (keen to start lawsuits) and courts were finding it hard to keep up with the volume of cases. Law professionals and scholars called a major conference (the Pound Conference of 1976[9]) where they proposed reforms to the American legal system, and some of these (such as alternative dispute resolution) were implemented. Since that time, the number of trials has declined steeply, prompting new concerns that too little litigation is also unhealthy both for law and society. Some observers fear that legal disputes involving important legal rights such as freedom from discrimination are being settled privately so that they have no impact on wider society. Legal scholars fret that trials and judgments are necessary to produce precedents that will keep the common law relevant and useful. In relation to criminal litigation, it is probable that the volume of cases entering the legal system depends significantly upon the level of police activity, a response to people's attitudes toward crime and their willingness to pay for enforcement of the law. The "optimal" amount of litigation will remain a contentious issue in any society that seeks a balance between the needs of its people and the responsiveness of its legal systems.

After reading this chapter you should be able to:

- explain what is meant by social systems and how that concept has been criticized
- describe some features of the relationship between legal systems and society
- describe the doctrine of precedent and explain how it affects court systems
- list some of the functions of court and administrative systems
- explain what is meant by alternative systems and give examples of them
- research and describe the legal systems of a particular territorial jurisdiction

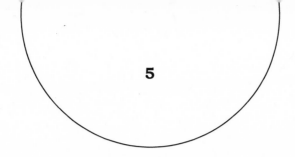

5

LEGAL PROCESSES AND PROCEDURES

Planning and Procedures for Processes
used by Legal Institutions

We do not plan to be in a car accident or to have a flood in our house, but both events, and others like them, may involve us in legal situations that will require careful planning. If our car insurance company rejects a claim for the loss of a computer that went missing at the time of the accident, or the water company will not take responsibility for a defective sewer system, we may need to start legal proceedings. Because there are many steps on the path to justice, legal planning will give us the best chance of obtaining a favourable result whether we are involved in litigation or other legal activities. Legal planning will be useful both for the purpose of achieving everyday legal objectives such as making a will and opening a business, and in rarer situations such as seeking judgment from a court or tribunal. This chapter is concerned primarily with the processes and procedures of decision-makers when resolving legal disputes. Planning for and following the required steps in litigation is like reading and deciphering a map of the road to justice.

Studies in many jurisdictions have found that most people do not understand legal processes and procedures very well. Mass media is partly to blame, by focusing on trials without showing the laborious investigation, documentation, and preparation that leads up to them. It is therefore under-standable that people may expect to commence a claim and get a decision from a judge without any delay. Actual legal procedures are not only unglamorous for TV viewing, they are also complex and numerous. Ronald W. Staudt and Paula L. Hannaford studied civil litigation procedures in the United States, and found 193 discrete functions, such as "interpret law," "develop strategy," or "negotiate," that a disputant must carry out to make the civil litigation system work.[1] Many courts and agencies now try to assist people without lawyers to navigate this procedural maze by providing checklists, automated court docu-ment preparation systems, workshops for litigants, and other forms of support. Nevertheless, planning and undertaking a legal case remains demanding. As observed in the United Kingdom, an individual managing and planning legal matters must: understand process and procedures; identify and avoid risks; plan ahead; manage relationships and negotiate; and be motivated to act and be persistent.[2]

One of the chief advantages enjoyed by lawyers and litigating parties such as insurance companies and banks is intimate knowledge of the processes and procedures of law, which they gain through training and repeat experience. These experienced actors not only know what to do when, but can plan ahead to arrange their affairs in order to secure the best possible result should a legal problem arise. Large corporations, governments, and businesses that litigate as part of their normal operations can adopt strategic plans including legal steps to further their long-range interests. Such litigants plan ahead to be involved in lawsuits; they arrange their business affairs to have the best chance of win-ning. Businesses may also use litigation as marketing by other means when they protect their own patents and trademarks in court and challenge those of their competitors. Frequent litigants can also plan their interaction with courts to obtain the optimum results averaged over a number of individual disputes without needing to win all cases. Such a strategy may favour the settlement of strong claims in order to avoid setting adverse precedents, and unbend-ing opposition to weak ones in order to obtain favourable precedents from the courts. Computer programs have been developed to assist in planning and managing litigation and other legal matters.[3] The patent by Heckman and his colleagues in figure 5.1 provides a glimpse of how litigation planning can be done using an automated case processing system.

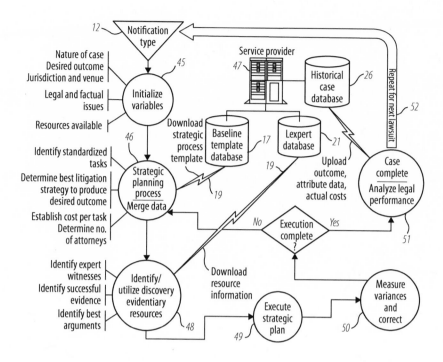

Figure 5.1 Diagram of patent for automatic case processing system.

In contrast, people who infrequently encounter law are at a distinct disadvantage because they not only lack knowledge of what to do when but they are also unprepared because they usually have not planned ahead for the contingency of becoming involved in legal proceedings.

CIVIL LITIGATION PROCESS

It is important to be careful when using the word *civil* in connection with law; the word is sometimes used to describe legal systems based on *civil codes* (legislation such as found in France and Germany) which use the *inquisitorial* process, in contrast to systems based on common law (such as in the United Kingdom and Canada) which use the *adversarial* process. Thus, lawyers speak of *civil law systems* and *common law systems* to describe legal systems at the national level. (Note that the province of Québec in Canada has a civil law system in provincial law as a result of its French heritage.) Another distinction made in the law is between *criminal proceedings* and all others which are called *civil cases*. Finally, the word civil is also sometimes used to differentiate between military (martial) and non-military (civil) law and processes. Thus, we have *courts martial* (courts applying military law) and *martial law* as distinct from the civil law system that applies to civilians (non-military persons). "Civil" is thus an example of an ordinary word that has been given unique and multiple meanings in law. This problem and others that contribute to the difficulty of legal language will be considered in the next chapter.

Within common law systems, non-criminal proceedings follow the civil litigation process. Civil *process and procedure* is different from *criminal process and procedure*. You will also find that the word "process" is sometimes used to describe a legal document notice of which must be given to someone, what is known as *service of process* (giving notice with a legal document), a task performed by the *process server* (person who delivers the notice). Process is important to people in disputes, sometimes even more than the final outcome. This is the finding of a large body of research based on the concept of *procedural justice*. If people view legal procedures as being fair, they are also likely to be more trustful of the legal system, which contributes to its legitimacy in the eyes of the public.

Researchers have identified several features that the public expects from procedural justice. John Thibaut and Laurens Walker proposed that people are concerned with how much control they have within the procedures they must follow, and distinguished control over the process itself from control over the result.[4] In situations where there is a *conflict of interest* they proposed that the parties should have a high degree of control over the process, but not over the final decision. In situations where the dispute is primarily a *conflict of facts*, they suggested both elements of control are best left with an impartial *third party* (judge or adjudicator). Tom Tyler's research showed that people evaluate the perceived motives and ethics (including respectfulness) of officials when evaluating the fairness of procedures.[5] These requirements of procedural justice are one way to evaluate legal processes and procedures. A critical legal studies perspective can be used to examine common civil litigation processes with this in mind.

Just as legal structures and systems are focused on courts and judges, legal process is focused on trials in which judges preside. In a common law adversarial system, a trial is a single, continuous oral *hearing* at which the disputing parties (or their lawyers) present all of their *evidence* (information about disputed facts), and make their *arguments* (also called *submissions*). At the conclusion of a trial, the judge makes a decision either immediately (oral judgment) or judgment is *reserved* (to be delivered later). (In an inquisitorial system, judgment is arrived at through a series of hearings in which the judge relies mostly on written records.) The civil litigation process is therefore the series of steps taken for the purpose of preparing for a trial. It also includes those steps to be taken if a judgment given at trial is appealed to a higher court.

In an adversarial litigation process, the disputing parties are responsible for taking the required steps, subject to supervision by a judge, who settles disputes over whether the proper procedure has been followed. The responsibility placed on the parties continues at trial, where each side chooses the evidence they wish to present to the judge. An adversarial legal process therefore resembles a tennis match where one side takes a step toward trial and triggers the other to respond.

In an inquisitorial system, the judge is the one who takes the steps leading to judgment, and who obtains and selects the evidence used in making the decision. Another difference between the two types of process is that a jury may be used in adversarial proceedings, but usually not in inquisitorial ones. Juries, however, are becoming rarer in common law jurisdictions. Processes in adversarial and inquisitorial courts are becoming more alike as a result of common law judges gaining more powers to manage the conduct of litigation, chiefly for the purpose of speeding up the process. This innovation in adversarial processes has been called *managerial judging*.

There are four basic stages in the adversarial version of civil legal process:

1. *Pleading*—the preparation and filing of documents with the court that describe the claims made and the legal issues in dispute, and the written response by the other side.

2. *Discovery*—mutual disclosure by the parties of information that may be presented as evidence at trial, often accompanied by written or oral questioning of the other side to gain further information.

3. *Trial*—or *settlement* without trial by agreement between the parties.

4. *Appeal*—asking a higher court to overrule (reverse) an incorrect judgment.

The function of the pleading and discovery stages are to prepare a record of the legal issues to be decided at the trial, and to give each party notice of the evidence that will be presented by the other side. Since the beginning of the twentieth century, more emphasis has been placed by the courts on the disclosure (discovery) process in order to prevent what has been called *trial by ambush*. This term describes the situation where one party becomes aware of evidence for the first time at trial, and is therefore unprepared to present contrary evidence in response. The surprised party may lose the case or have to request an *adjournment* (temporary halt) of the trial, causing delay and increased expense.

Although it is designed to avert trial by ambush, the process of discovery has itself been criticized for being unjust and inefficient. It is often prolonged, and generates a significant proportion of lawyers' fees in many lawsuits. Lawyers have been accused of using discovery to wear down opponents with endless requests for information and documents, and of abusing parties through oral pretrial questioning (known as *examination for discovery*). Perhaps more inquisitorial intervention by judges will help to avoid these problems.

Procedural rules direct the parties in what they must do as they move through the stages of the civil litigation process toward trial. They are the subject of the next section.

CIVIL PROCEDURE

Procedures for civil litigation are usually set by the *rules of court* adopted by judges within a particular jurisdiction.* Parties to a lawsuit are expected to follow these rules in preparing for trial, and disputes about whether someone has followed the rules are decided by judges who issue *interlocutory* orders (those rendered before final judgment). The purpose of procedural rules is to ensure that litigation is conducted "in accordance with the principles of fundamental justice."[6] The Constitution of the United States includes a similar requirement that legal proceedings follow due process.

---

* The examples in this section are taken from the *Alberta Rules of Court* in force from November 2010. They are based on extensive study and careful revision; accordingly, they reflect current recommended best practice for common law courts. Further, an attempt has been made to express them in plain language.

Purpose and intention of these rules

1.2(1) The purpose of these rules is to provide a means by which claims can be fairly and justly resolved in or by a court process in a timely and cost-effective way.[7]

Courts accept that if strict application of a procedural rule would, in certain circumstances, go against these fundamental principles, then the rule should be waived or its requirements relaxed. Judges have the power to enforce rules of court in a flexible way, but must always keep the rights of both parties in mind. In some cases, it may be unfair to the other side to excuse one party from following the rules.

Rule contravention, non-compliance and irregularities

1.5(1) If a person contravenes or does not comply with these rules, or if there is an irregularity in a commencement document, pleading, document, affidavit or prescribed form, a party may apply to the Court

(a) to cure the contravention, non-compliance or irregularity.
. . .

(4) The Court must not cure any contravention, non-compliance or irregularity unless

(a) to do so will cause no irreparable harm to any party,

Note: Here, "cure" means to reverse any adverse effects of not complying with a rule.

A look at the table of contents of the *Alberta Rules* shows that they are basically organized in chronological order, following the stages of the civil litigation process. In the pleading stage they set out how parties are to be selected, identified, and named.

Actions by and against sole proprietors

2.5 (1) If a person carries on business or operates as a sole proprietor under a name other than the person's name, the person may bring or be the subject of an action in that name.

(2) If an action is brought by or against a person in the person's business or operating name, a party may serve a notice requiring the person to disclose, in writing, the legal name of the person carrying on the business or operation.

A plaintiff begins a lawsuit (an *action*) by preparing, filing, and serving a *Statement of Claim* (or just *Claim*), and the defendant responds in the same way with a *Statement of Defence* (or just *Defence*). The required contents of pleadings are specified to ensure the other side is not taken by surprise.

Pleadings: general requirements

13.6 (2) A pleading must state any of the following matters that are relevant:

    (a) the facts on which a party relies, but not the evidence by which the facts are to be proved;

    (b) a matter that defeats, or raises a defence to, a claim of another party;

    (c) the remedy claimed, including

        (i) the type of damages* claimed,

        (ii) to the extent known, the amount of general and special damages claimed, or if either or both are not known, an estimate of the amount or the total amount that will be claimed,

        (iii) a statement of any interest claimed, including the basis for the interest, and the method of calculating the interest, and

        (iv) costs,** including any known special costs.

(3) A pleading must also include a statement of any matter on which a party intends to rely that may take another party by surprise. . . .

*Damages are an amount of money to be awarded as compensation; general damages are an estimate, with the final amount decided by the judge; special damages are exact amounts already spent or lost by a party.

**Costs are those expenses of pursuing the lawsuit that the court allows the successful party to collect from the other side. They usually do not cover all of the expenses of hiring a lawyer. Special costs are exact sums of money that have been paid, such as medical expenses and fees.

Rules of court always provide that pleadings should be *served* (delivered) to opposing parties to ensure they have adequate notice of every step in the proceedings and sufficient time to respond.

The *Alberta Rules* adopt the approach of *managerial judging* by stipulating that the parties have the primary responsibility to prepare for trial expeditiously, but that the court also has a role in managing the litigation process.

Ways the Court may manage action

4.11 The Court may manage an action in one or more of the following ways, in which case the responsibility of the parties to manage their dispute is modified accordingly:

(a) the Court may make a procedural order;

(b) the Court may direct a conference under rule 4.10 [Assistance by the Court];

(c) on request under rule 4.12 [Request for case management], or on the initiative of the Chief Justice under rule 4.13 [Appointment of case management judge], the Chief Justice may appoint a case management judge for the action;

(d) the Court may make an order under a rule providing for specific direction or a remedy.

Rules, such as producing records held by one party, that define the permissible scope of requests for information place limits on the discovery stage of litigation.

When something is relevant and material

5.2 (1) For the purposes of this Part, a question, record or information is relevant and material only if the answer to the question, or the record or information, could reasonably be expected

(a) to significantly help determine one or more of the issues raised in the pleadings, or

(b) to ascertain evidence that could reasonably be expected to significantly help determine one or more of the issues raised in the pleadings.

Procedure at trial is governed by rules specifying the order in which the parties should present their evidence and argument.

Order of presentation

8.10 (1) Unless the Court directs otherwise, the order of presentation at a trial is as follows:

(a) the plaintiff may make one opening statement and, subject to clause (b), must then adduce evidence;

(b) the defendant may make one opening statement either immediately after the plaintiff's opening statement and before the plaintiff adduces evidence, or at the conclusion of the plaintiff's evidence;

(c) when the plaintiff's evidence is concluded, the defendant may make an opening statement if the defendant has not already done so immediately after the plaintiff's opening statement, and the defendant must then adduce evidence, if any;

(d) when the defendant's evidence is concluded, the plaintiff may adduce evidence, if any, to rebut the defendant's evidence;

(e) when the defendant's evidence and the plaintiff's rebuttal evidence, if any, are concluded, the plaintiff may make a closing statement, followed by the defendant's closing statement, after which the plaintiff may reply;

(f) if the defendant adduces no evidence after the conclusion of the plaintiff's evidence, the plaintiff may make a closing statement, followed by the defendant's closing statement, after which the plaintiff may reply.

Rules regarding appeals specify how they are to be commenced and what documents must be filed with the appeal court. Other rules of court concern matters such as how documents should be prepared; how documents are to be served; procedures to compel witnesses to appear at trial; and how the costs of the proceedings and the lawyers are dealt with. The examples from the Alberta Rules are representative of typical rules of court concerning the main stages in the civil litigation process—pleading, discovery, trial, and appeal.. Today, the rules of most courts are available online.

CRIMINAL LITIGATION PROCESS

Before moving into the criminal litigation process, a few comments on terminology are in order. The party who starts a civil lawsuit is called a *plaintiff*, and the party who is sued is called a *defendant*. In criminal matters, the party who commences the proceedings (a police officer or government lawyer) brings a charge against an *accused* (the person alleged to have committed a criminal offence). The initiating party in criminal litigation is called the *prosecutor* or, in countries such as Canada for whom the Queen is the head of state, the Crown.

In legal documents, the Crown is usually referred to by the Latin name, *Regina* (Queen). This is why the title of documents relating to criminal cases takes the form of *R.* (*Regina*) v. *X* (the Crown versus the accused, "X"). (The word versus is not used when speaking of court cases—"and" is substituted instead, as in "The Crown and X".)

Now, in its basic format, the criminal litigation process in common law systems is essentially the same as the civil version. The adversarial process normally requires an oral trial where witnesses testify in person before the judge and may be questioned by all parties. This type of proceeding is more appropriate for criminal matters because the stakes are higher for those involved. The prospect of conviction and imprisonment can lead people to be dishonest and tamper with witnesses—these things are less likely to occur in civil proceedings. A common law adversarial trial that allows *cross-examination* of witnesses (questioning by an opposing party) is thought to be very effective in testing the *credibility* (believability) of witnesses' testimony (oral statements in court). This type of trial process is therefore useful for discovering the truth (or more accurately, who is lying) about criminal acts. The same type of process may not be necessary in many civil proceedings.

There is, however, one significant difference between civil and criminal legal proceedings. In criminal matters one side is the state, which has immense resources (such as detectives, wiretaps, and forensic scientists) at its disposal. The accused is often a single, frequently poor, individual with few resources and no lawyer. The "scales of justice" appear to be weighted heavily in favour of the state facing such an ill-equipped adversary. For this reason, most Western countries have adopted laws governing criminal litigation processes that are intended to give an accused person a better opportunity for a fair trial. These laws do not apply to civil proceedings. Laws benefiting an accused person reflect the legal system's historical role as protector of the individual against official power.

Countries such as Canada and the United States have provisions within their constitutions that apply only to criminal matters. They are designed to help make criminal proceedings a more level playing field between the prosecution and the accused. Canada's Charter of Rights and Freedoms states in part:

Arrest or detention

10. Everyone has the right on arrest or detention

(a) to be informed promptly of the reasons therefore;

(b) to retain and instruct counsel without delay and to be informed of that right; and

(c) to have the validity of the detention determined by way of habeas corpus* and to be released if the detention is not lawful.

Proceedings in criminal and penal matters

11. Any person charged with an offence has the right

(a) to be informed without unreasonable delay of the specific offence;

(b) to be tried within a reasonable time;

(c) not to be compelled to be a witness in proceedings against that person in respect of the offence;

(d) to be presumed innocent until proven guilty according to law in a fair and public hearing by an independent and impartial tribunal.

*habeas corpus is a request made to a court for an order to release a person from custody.

Because these protections and assurances are in the constitution they go beyond mere procedure, and become substantive rights that an accused person can insist on. Unlike rules of court, judges have no authority to waive these provisions or apply them flexibly. These legal requirements are part of the foundation of the criminal litigation process. As further protection for an accused person, the evidence must be sufficient to prove they are guilty *beyond a reasonable doubt*. This *standard of proof* (degree of certainty) is higher than it is for civil proceedings, where a *balance of probabilities* (more probable than not) is sufficient to prove facts. Although the criminal standard of proof is not expressly stated in the Canadian Constitution, it has such a long tradition in common law systems that it is considered binding in all courts.

Another protection for accused persons that has been adopted in many Western countries is the right to have a lawyer paid for by the state when charged with a serious offence. When people wish to represent themselves (or act *pro se* in U.S. terminology) in criminal proceedings, judges may need to intervene more actively to ensure a fair trial. Judges may also be inclined to forgive some errors in following correct procedure made by the accused to make sure a *self-represented* accused person is not treated unfairly because he or she lacks knowledge of law and legal process.

One difference between civil and criminal processes is that the victim harmed by a crime is not a named party in the criminal proceedings, which are solely between the state and the accused. In a civil proceeding where one party seeks compensation for injuries inflicted during a crime, the victim is a plaintiff and entitled to take full part in the process and trial. Not including the victim in criminal processes has been described as a failure of the legal system that harms both victims and offenders. The movements for *therapeutic jurisprudence* (legal processes concerned with healing rather than retribution) and *restorative justice* (rebuilding a community disrupted by crime) have sought to bring victims (and offenders) into the criminal process in new ways by giving them a more active role and voice. This is one response to the problem of access to justice for victims of crime.

Finally, *problem-solving courts* (courts that address underlying social issues) and *drug courts* (courts created to deal with the special problems associated with drug addiction) are advocated by those who wish to see changes in the criminal litigation process. Rather than focusing on punishment, the advocates of such courts envisage a legal process that involves the surrounding community in addition to individual victims, in an attempt to understand and deal with some of the underlying reasons for criminal behaviour.

CRIMINAL PROCEDURE

Courts generally apply the same rules of procedure in criminal cases that they do in civil ones, so far as they are relevant, and unless there are other special rules provided by law. Specific rules of procedure for criminal cases are set out for instance in Canada in the Criminal Code, Parts XV to XXII. The following are some examples from the Code that illustrate how the adversarial process is directed in criminal litigation.

The document prepared to start a criminal process in Canada is called an *information*, based upon which an accused person may be *summonsed* (ordered) to appear in court or arrested and brought there. An information is the criminal law equivalent to the statement of claim that commences a civil proceeding.

In what cases justice may receive information

504. Anyone who, on reasonable grounds, believes that a person has committed an indictable offence may lay an information in writing and under oath before a justice, and the justice shall receive the information, where it is alleged

(a) that the person has committed, anywhere, an indictable offence that may be tried in the province in which the justice resides, and that the person

(i) is or is believed to be, or

(ii) resides or is believed to reside,
within the territorial jurisdiction of the justice;

(b) that the person, wherever he may be, has committed an indictable offence within the territorial jurisdiction of the justice;

(c) that the person has, anywhere, unlawfully received property that was unlawfully obtained within the territorial jurisdiction of the justice; or

(d) that the person has in his possession stolen property within the territorial jurisdiction of the justice.[8]

In serious cases, the criminal process in Canada may include a *preliminary inquiry* (hearing before trial) where witnesses are called. This procedure enables a judge to decide whether there is sufficient evidence to justify proceeding to full trial. A preliminary hearing is also an opportunity for the accused to benefit from disclosure of the evidence that will be used against him; it is therefore also a form of discovery in criminal cases. Even though a preliminary inquiry is not held, the prosecution must still disclose to the accused the evidence to be presented at trial, with some restrictions related to sexual offences where certain kinds of evidence may be withheld. A judge may also order the prosecution to provide *particulars* (details of the facts the prosecution will rely on) to the accused before trial, another form of disclosure.

Statement of issues and witnesses

536.3 If a request for a preliminary inquiry is made, the prosecutor or, if the request was made by the accused, counsel for the accused shall, within the period fixed by rules of court made under section 482 or 482.1 or, if there are no such rules, by the justice, provide the court and the other party with a statement that identifies

(a) the issues on which the requesting party wants evidence to be given at the inquiry; and

(b) the witnesses that the requesting party wants to hear at the inquiry.

Further provisions allow the accused to inspect the evidence and exhibits to be presented at trial.

Prior to trial, the prosecution is required to prepare an *indictment*, a final statement of the charge (or charges) for which the accused will stand trial. This may incorporate a charge not originally included in the information based on evidence given at a preliminary inquiry. The indictment is equivalent to a more detailed pleading in civil procedure.

Substance of offence

581.(1) Each count in an indictment shall in general apply to a single transaction and shall contain in substance a statement that the accused or defendant committed an offence therein specified.

Form of statement

(2) The statement referred to in subsection (1) may be

(a) in popular language without technical averments or allegations of matters that are not essential to be proved;

(b) in the words of the enactment that describes the offence or declares the matters charged to be an indictable offence; or

(c) in words that are sufficient to give to the accused notice of the offence with which he is charged.

Details of circumstances

(3) A count shall contain sufficient detail of the circumstances of the alleged offence to give to the accused reasonable information with respect to the act or omission to be proved against him and to identify the transaction referred to, but otherwise the absence or insufficiency of details does not vitiate the count.

The accused is not required to put his or her defence in writing—an oral *plea* (statement of position) of not guilty is sufficient.

Procedure at a criminal trial is similar to civil proceedings, with some specific directions to the judge regarding the order of presentations. The following rules are to be followed at a preliminary hearing, and also apply during a trial.

Hearing of witnesses

541.(1) When the evidence of the witnesses called on the part of the prosecution has been taken down and, where required by this Part, has been read, the justice shall, subject to this section, hear the witnesses called by the accused.

Contents of address to accused

(2) Before hearing any witness called by an accused who is not represented by counsel, the justice shall address the accused as follows or to the like effect:

> "Do you wish to say anything in answer to these charges or to any other charges which might have arisen from the evidence led by the prosecution? You are not obliged to say anything, but whatever you do say may be given in evidence against you at your trial. You should not make any confession or admission of guilt because of any promise or threat made to you, but if you do make any statement it may be given in evidence against you at your trial in spite of the promise or threat."

Statement of accused

(3) Where the accused who is not represented by counsel says anything in answer to the address made by the justice pursuant to subsection (2), the answer shall be taken down in writing and shall be signed by the justice and kept with the evidence of the witnesses and dealt with in accordance with this Part.

Witnesses for accused

(4) Where an accused is not represented by counsel, the justice shall ask the accused if he or she wishes to call any witnesses after subsections (2) and (3) have been complied with.

Depositions of such witnesses

(5) The justice shall hear each witness called by the accused who testifies to any matter relevant to the inquiry, and for the purposes of this subsection, section 540 applies with such modifications as the circumstances require.

Confession or admission of accused

542. (1) Nothing in this Act prevents a prosecutor giving in evidence at a preliminary inquiry any admission, confession or statement made at any time by the accused that by law is admissible against him.

At trial, the *laws of evidence* (rules about what evidence may be presented) give some protection to an accused person. In particular, evidence obtained illegally may be excluded in order to encourage lawful behaviour in state officials.

A recent addition to criminal procedure is the giving of *victim statements* at the end of proceedings, intended to help the court set an appropriate punishment by taking into account the harm that has been done by the crime.

Appeal procedures in criminal matters are similar to those in civil cases, except that the prosecution can only appeal issues of law, and not questions of fact that have been decided at trial.[9]

ADMINISTRATIVE PROCESSES AND PROCEDURES

Paul R. Verkuil, referring to the American context, suggests that 90 percent of what government does in relation to the individual can be described as "informal adjudication."[10] This statistic is probably also correct for most other Western countries such as Canada. Verkuil also provides a list of types of government action that shows the range of issues and situations subject to administrative processes and procedures:

1. Imposition of sanctions (penalties).

2. Ratemaking, licensing, and other regulatory decisions.

3. Environmental and safety decisions.

4. Awards of benefits, loans, grants, and subsidies.

5. Inspections, audits, and approvals.

6. Planning and policy-making.[11]

The challenge for a legal system is to adopt processes and procedures that are effective for this wide variety of governmental action, while being fair enough to be considered legitimate by the public. One question to be decided when a government creates tribunals and other quasi-judicial bodies is whether adversarial processes are suitable for administrative contexts. For some purposes, such as claiming workers' compensation, an inquisitorial process has been adopted in many jurisdictions. This allows a tribunal hearing such claims to take active steps to discover and use information regarding accidents and injuries without waiting for the parties involved to act. However, when an administrative decision primarily affects the opposing interests of two or more members of the public, as in disputes over zoning and building (development), then a more adversarial process is often appropriate.

The Alberta Law Reform Institute has identified some of the principles that should guide the design of administrative processes and procedures:

- flexibility; tribunals should be able to mould their process to suit their particular needs
- inquisitorial powers may be appropriate for some purposes
- processes and procedures must remain fair and just
- efficiency of operation is to be taken into account
- processes and procedures must be effective.[12]

Courts have a supervisory role over administrative processes and procedures to ensure they follow the basic requirements of procedural justice. In Canada, an administrative decision may be challenged in court in two ways: through *judicial review* (examination of the record of the proceeding by a judge), or by appeal of the decision to the courts, where a right of appeal is given by law. The judgments of the courts in such cases provide guidance to administrative agencies. In particular, the courts determine what level of procedural informality will be compatible with procedural justice. Over the years, Canadian courts have expanded the description of types of administrative action that must follow these principles, but judges continue to recognize the need for flexibility and informality in administrative procedures: "the nature and extent of the procedural protections that the Court is willing to recognize are varied and depend on the nature and context of the statutory or prerogative power in issue."[13]

Many jurisdictions now have legislation that sets out the procedural steps to be followed by administrative agencies when making quasi-judicial decisions that affect the public. The *Administrative Procedures and Jurisdiction Act* of Alberta, an instance of this type of law, will be used in the following examples.[14]

The first essential element of fair administrative procedure is that everyone who may be affected by a decision should be notified in advance of making it. (In civil litigation, this is done by the service of process described above.)

Notice to parties

3. When
   (a) an application is made to an authority, or
   (b) an authority on its own initiative proposes

to exercise a statutory power, the authority shall give to all
parties adequate notice of the application that it has before it or
of the power that it intends to exercise.

The next step is to disclose the information the administrative body will use
in making its decision (equivalent to discovery in civil proceedings) and give
effect to the parties' *right to be heard* (give evidence and make arguments as in
a civil trial).

Evidence and representations

4. Before an authority, in the exercise of a statutory power,
refuses the application of or makes a decision or order adversely
affecting the rights of a party, the authority

   (a) shall give the party a reasonable opportunity of
   furnishing relevant evidence to the authority,

   (b) shall inform the party of the facts in its possession or the
   allegations made to it contrary to the interests of the party
   in sufficient detail

      (i) to permit the party to understand the facts or
      allegations, and

      (ii) to afford the party a reasonable opportunity to furnish
      relevant evidence to contradict or explain the facts or
      allegations,

   and

   (c) shall give the party an adequate opportunity of making
   representations by way of argument to the authority.

The Alberta Act goes on to provide that representations need not be made orally if written material is adequate, and there is no absolute right to cross-examine any witness, which would always be allowed in a civil trial.

Finally, the act requires a decision to be made in writing (corresponding to a judgment following trial).

> Written decision with reasons
>
> 7. When an authority exercises a statutory power so as to adversely affect the rights of a party, the authority shall furnish to each party a written statement of its decision setting out
>
>> (a) the findings of fact on which it based its decision, and
>> (b) the reasons for the decision.

The legal provisions above are examples of how the desire for flexibility in administrative decision-making has been reconciled with the need to maintain its legitimacy by providing fair and just procedures.

The overall process of notice, followed by disclosure, participation in a hearing, and receiving a decision is similar to that followed in civil and criminal litigation. Administrative proceedings, however, typically have fewer detailed rules about how these steps are to be taken.

CRITICAL ANALYSIS OF PROCESS AND PROCEDURE

The terms *process* and *procedure* are often used interchangeably. In this chapter they have been used to refer to different things. Process means the sequence of operations (activities) that occur within the legal system when a person asserts or defends a legal right or obligation. Process is therefore a general description of the steps to be taken in a lawsuit. Procedure, in this chapter, describes the way operations in the legal system are carried out, usually according to rules. Rules of procedure give a more detailed description of what must be done in each step of a legal process.

Some have criticized adversarial legal processes for being inappropriate, ineffective (or counter-productive), and inefficient. Although not inevitable, the adversarial process does have a tendency to stimulate aggressiveness and hostility in the disputing parties. These effects are considered particularly inappropriate in situations such as family disputes where the needs of children are in question, and some form of continuing relationship between the parents is required. Carla Hotel and Joan Brockman found that family lawyers fall within a "conciliatory-adversarial" continuum in relation to how they viewed their roles.[15] More conciliatory lawyers took "a contextual approach to finding a solution to a legal problem [taking] into account the relationship between the parties" while adversarial-oriented lawyers "focused on the duty to their clients and their clients' rights."[16] Other critics have suggested that in family matters, the adversarial process is especially hurtful to children because it tends to ignore their interests and instead focusses on the conflict between parents.

Certain groups have promoted alternative dispute resolution processes such as mediation, in which lawyers play a lesser role, because they believe these do not stir up the same competitiveness and hostility as adversarial litigation. Lawyers themselves have responded to criticism by adopting new forms of practice such as *collaborative law* or *cooperative law* in a deliberate attempt to counter adversarialism. Collaborative family lawyers agree with their clients to represent them in negotiations but not in a trial, thus shunning the adversarial process completely.

Other critics of the adversarial legal process note that it forces the parties to take polarized positions and present contradictory evidence, when the truth probably lies somewhere in between. According to this critique, a truly just result would take each side's interests (needs and aspirations) into account. Adversarial proceedings that require a choice between competing arguments (the debating model) do not allow the subtleties of the parties' different perspectives to emerge. As Carrie Menkel-Meadow puts it, "the negative and reactive thinking produced by adversarial argument may limit more open ways of conceptualizing solutions to problems."[17]

Another commonly recognized failing of the adversarial process is how it encourages expert witnesses (such as doctors or engineers) to be biased according to who has employed them and therefore less useful to a judge when deciding a technical issue. Rather than being the best route to finding the truth, adversarial proceedings can exaggerate any uncertainties, require excessive amounts of evidence to be obtained and presented, and thus drive up the cost of litigation. The counter-argument to this problem is that putting the *burden of proof* (responsibility to present evidence) on the parties in the adversary system results in more useful information being presented to the decision-maker than in inquisitorial models. These are the ongoing debates about whether the adversarial process is an efficient one for determining facts and resolving disputes.

Some have also criticized legal procedure itself. As a set of detailed rules, it is another level of law that must be mastered before the *merits* (real matters in dispute) of a lawsuit can be brought before a judge for decision. Disputes arise over whether procedural rules have been properly followed, resulting in delay and increased expense. Procedural technicalities can be used to wear the other party down so that settlement appears more attractive than trial.

Critics of legal procedure have called for more informal processes. Alternative dispute resolution procedures have become popular because of their informality compared to litigation. As Tom R. Tyler states, such alternative procedures "seek to serve the joint interest of society and the disputant in having swift and low-cost justice."[18] He goes on to suggest that some informal procedures also better meet the parties' desires to have a real voice in the process. In criminal processes, informality has been introduced through restorative justice initiatives that bring victims, offenders, and the surrounding community together outside the courtroom. Whether even these informal procedures can benefit from involvement of professionals such as lawyers is also a subject of debate.

Marc Galanter, in a classic article within law and society scholarship, describes the relative advantages of "repeat players" (those often involved in lawsuits) over "one-shotters" (those rarely involved in litigation).[19] One of the advantages enjoyed by repeat players is that they gain useful knowledge and experience of legal procedure, and they are often able to hire lawyers, who are also repeat players, to assist them. Galanter's concern about the fairness of legal processes is now shared by many; it is one focus of the access to justice movement.

The complexity and formality of legal procedures, and the advantage of having a lawyer to deal with them are aspects of the current legal system that challenge us again to consider its accessibility and responsiveness to the needs of society. Merely changing procedural rules may not, however, have the desired effect of increasing accessibility; this reality suggests another area where critical legal studies may contribute by analyzing and evaluating procedural innovations that may yield beneficial substantive results. Those who can plan to follow legal steps they understand have greater access to justice through law; this highlights the importance of legal literacy for developing people's capability to navigate the twists and turns of law's processes and procedures.

CHAPTER REVIEW

After reading this chapter you should be able to:

- explain some critiques of legal processes and procedures
- list some differences between adversarial and inquisitorial processes
- describe the main steps of a civil litigation process and explain the functions of each step
- describe the main steps of a criminal legal process and explain the functions of each step
- explain what is meant by an administrative justice process and describe its main features
- research and describe a legal process in a legal jurisdiction

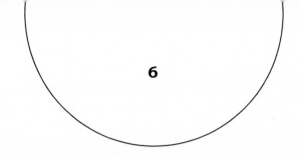

6

LEGAL LANGUAGE

Examining Language in Legal Institutions

Legal analysis or planning inevitably involves working with strange words (like "tort" and "pleading") plus common words used in new ways with unfamiliar meanings (such as "civil" and "damages"). A humorous story is sometimes told in legal circles about parties who are faced with the process of "execution," which in law means seizing someone's property to settle a debt they owe. But such terminology is not much of a joke to non-lawyers. The challenge of comprehending legal expression only increases when the time comes to do some legal research. In this chapter we look at legal language as an obstacle to understanding law from a critical legal studies perspective, and to the pursuit of justice for people who are not legal professionals.

Many have described law as having its own language, sometimes called *legalese*, and others have considered law to be a dialect within society.[1] As I discuss below, the language of the law is probably better described as a "creole," a distinct combination of other languages with its own life and development.

It is not only unique words, phrases, and uncommon meanings that distinguish legal language from everyday conversation or writing. As I discussed previously, the legal system claims to be at least semi-autonomous in relation to other social systems. One way the legal system promotes its autonomy and affirms its self-sufficiency is to require people making use of the law to adopt a unique terminology for expressing concepts, ideas, perspectives, and assumptions. Being able to communicate using this special language is a criterion for credible expression of legal ideas and arguments. This "policing" of communication results in limiting references and links to systems of thought outside law, and encourages development of a distinct self-referential context of communication for legal purposes. Legal communication thus occurs within a dense web of interrelated legal meanings and ideas which those outside the legal system find difficult to grasp.

LEGAL DISCOURSE

Legal discourse refers to the flow of communication with unique characteristics that occurs among people who operate the legal system. One feature of such discourse is the use of legal language, but those who study legal discourse look beyond the mere form of speech or writing to examine its effects, both within the legal system and on those outside it—that is, on society as a whole. This section examines how legal language is used to accomplish the purposes of lawyers, judges, and other "insiders" who are part of the legal system.[2]

First, it is important to note that language is both the tool and the product of the legal system. Words are its input and output. Certainly, physical actions may be taken as a consequence of legal decisions (imprisonment, foreclosure and sale of property, etc.) but they are justified and respected because of the language of judgments, not the physical power of judges. The power of the law lies in words. John M. Conley and William M. O'Barr put it this way, "language is not merely the vehicle through which legal power operates: in many vital respects, language is legal power. The abstraction we call power is at once the cause and effect of countless linguistic interactions taking place every day at every level of the legal system."

For this reason, one of the primary purposes of legal discourse is to maintain its own legitimacy and respect as a valued discourse in society. In the previous chapter I noted that the steps taken in legal processes are intended to fulfill public expectations of procedural justice. In the same way, legal discourse is expected to embody justice in words. The phrase "just words" can thus be read ambiguously to mean that legal discourse is merely words, but is also expected to produce words that are just—the language of justice.

What are the characteristics of legal discourse that set it off from ordinary speech and writing? One key feature is that the discourse of law presents concepts and ideas such as *authority* and *justice* as if they exist independently of law, as real forces in the world similar to gravity and magnetism. Legal discourse describes itself as searching for, finding, and giving effect to such forces. Another way of describing this activity is to say that it involves *reifying* (creating objects out of) concepts. Critics label these effects as word games played either by deluded or deceptive lawyers and judges. Either the members of the legal system just do not realize that they are actually creating what they claim to be searching for, or they do know, and use legal discourse to reinforce their own power in society. We might say that legal discourse is therefore about imaginary objects, or more suspiciously, used to mystify outsiders. Thus, concepts such as justice should be considered figments of the imagination or political slogans (or both). Perhaps legal discourse reifies justice to mask its insubstantiality in an effort to reassure the public.

Another feature of legal discourse is what Peter Goodrich calls its "unity, coherence and univocality."[3] According to orthodox legal theory, all the law (at least for a specific territorial jurisdiction) forms a logical whole that is internally consistent, coherent, and self-sufficient. In other words, all the knowledge required to render justice is contained in the law and expressed by legal discourse. For Goodrich, this is a false claim. He argues that legal discourse is inescapably *rhetorical* (intended to persuade)—it is a discourse that attempts to convince everyone the results of legal decisions are inevitable, and that mere arguments can be transformed by the magical words of the law into legal certainties.

A third characteristic of legal discourse scholars have noted is its "poetic" quality. Here poetic is not used in the sense of being imaginatively appealing or playfully provocative, but dense and self-referential, like the self-contained world expressed by a good poem. One legal term is played off against another in a kind of dance of meaning that is familiar to the initiated but hard to follow by laypersons. Thus, legal discourse is embedded in multiple contexts and layers of significance that allows it to be read or spoken with a variety of meanings, like multiple interpretations of a poem. Although legal discourse is used to govern the "real world" it actually creates its own world of meaning in a way similar to creative writing.

Critics have identified adverse consequences of these features of legal discourse. According to William E. Conklin, the pain experienced by people who suffer legal wrongs is reconstituted in narratives that make sense in law, but do not truly reflect the feelings and desires of those it describes. He suggests that "the secondary legal discourse, as a result, strangely produces a suffering after one has allegedly been harmed."[4] Others have observed that the unique assumptions and conventions of legal discourse can disadvantage members of the public who do not communicate in the same way. When called upon to answer in court, members of some cultures may not respond in the way legal discourse considers credible, perhaps with hesitation or silence that is misinterpreted. Legal discourse can embody cultural or gendered prejudices that operate against the fair treatment of minorities and women within the legal system. Finally, we should also question whether the supposedly universal discourse of Western competition through rational debate in the adversarial system is truly adaptable to other cultural settings.

Sociolinguists who study law have discovered adverse effects of legal discourse in a variety of settings. Conley and O'Barr discuss research that shows how women are "re-victimized" by the language and procedures typically found in rape trials; how people may be manipulated through the discourse of mediators focused on settlement; and how legal discourse reflects predominantly male patterns of speech and behaviour.[5]

Many people also defend legal discourse. They believe that because doing justice is one of humanity's highest aspirations, a unique legal discourse is to be expected, and is perhaps inevitable. Just words (words embodying justice) should be somewhat different than ordinary language, much as poetry differs from prose. According to this view, justice is such a difficult and important concept that it warrants creating a special discourse with which to pursue it.

This discussion of legal discourse raises again the question of the nature of the relationship between law, the legal system, and the society they serve. Critical legal studies scholars working alongside those in other disciplines, such as linguistics and communication studies investigate whether legal discourse is of sufficient enough value in aiding the smooth operation of the legal system to outweigh its disadvantages to the public.

Legal language has a unique vocabulary that makes it different it from everyday speech and writing. This section explores legal vocabulary and its uniqueness.

One of the frequent criticisms of legal language is that it is often incomprehensible to the ordinary citizen because of its vocabulary. In one respect, however, legal language today may be an improvement on everyday language. This is in the area of *gender neutrality*. In the latter part of the twentieth century, feminists drew attention to the gendered vocabulary of the law, such as using "he" to mean both genders. The traditional approach was to legally define such masculine terms to "include" the female gender. Critics pointed out that "inclusion" of subordinated women did not treat the sexes equally. Law, they said, should practice what it preached and embody gender equality in its language since it declared parity to be a human right. In response to such criticism, lawyers and judges were encouraged and educated to change their vocabulary. It appears that these efforts have been successful according to a recent study of decisions in United States courts. Judith D. Fischer states, "professionals in many fields recognize that gender-biased language makes women invisible and constructs an inaccurate world. While some commentators express concerns that gender-neutral language will be awkward or annoying, language experts identify graceful ways to surmount these obstacles. The use of gender-neutral language has increased in many fields, including the legal profession."[6]

Some of the "graceful ways" to employ gender-neutral writing that Fischer identifies are: using plurals so that "they" (instead of "he") is appropriate; avoiding the need for pronouns ("a person who"); and using paired pronouns ("her or his"). Finally, she makes the point that judges today have largely come to expect gender-neutral language, so people should strive to use it when presenting arguments to them. Using gender-neutral vocabulary is one aspect of legal language today that should be emulated in ordinary writing.

Other aspects of legal vocabulary are unique to the history and functions of legal language. One result of the history of legal language is the use of many foreign words that often do not retain the same meaning as in their original language. This occurs also in ordinary speech and writing because English has frequently incorporated words from other languages. Just think of "percent," "quorum," and "post mortem," from Latin, and "RSVP," "allege," and "entrée" from French. But legal language uses foreign terms that are not found often, if at all, outside legal discourse.

Modern legal language is actually based on three languages: Old English (and other Anglo-Saxon languages), Latin, and French. This heritage reflects the history of English law, on which common law legal systems are based. Until the Norman conquest of England in 1066, laws were expressed in the local Anglo-Saxon dialects. The Normans brought with them one language of the continent, a dialect of French. As lawmakers, they began writing legislation in their own language, which was in turn adopted by lawyers and adapted to their own purposes. This was the beginning of what is known as *Law French*.

Law French quickly became less like French and more like legalese. French words were pronounced as if they were English, and given legal meanings not found in ordinary French. Some Law French words were also incorporated into ordinary English language, although many still have unique alternative meanings in law. Some examples of such words with a French origin are: *attorney* (person authorized to act for another or, in the United States, a lawyer), *bailiff* (officer of the court engaged in enforcement), *estate* (property left at death or type of landholding), *mortgage* (creditor's claim to land of the debtor) and *venue* (place of trial of a legal case). Other Law French words are only found in legal discourse: *cestui que trust* (beneficiary of a trust), *en banc* (group of judges hearing a case together), *estoppel* (being prevented from denying something), and *voir dire* (questioning someone before proceeding with a trial). One famous Law French word still used is *Oyez* (let us hear). This call is announced three times at the beginning of sittings of the United States Supreme Court.

The final language that has contributed words to the legal vocabulary is Latin. As the language of the church in the Middle Ages, Latin was considered authoritative and was adopted by the courts as their language of record. Documents filed in court were in Latin, resulting in standard forms of pleadings in legal proceedings. If a claim could not be fitted into Latin, then it could not be pursued. The effect of Latin forms has continued to the present day. Some legal proceedings still go by Latin names: *habeas corpus* (deliver up the person) and *certiorari* (certify the record of a hearing for review). In 1992, the High Court of Australia had to struggle with the common law concept of *terra nullius* (nobody's land) when considering whether it was possible to recognize the existence of Aboriginal title.[7]

Here are some other important Latin terms still forming part of legal language: *ab initio* (from the beginning), *ex parte* (without notice), *mandamus* (required to act), *mens rea* (intent to do something), and *pro se* (acting without a lawyer). The terms *pro bono*, or *pro bono publico* (for the public good) have also entered ordinary language as meaning a voluntary unpaid act. Lawyers are frequently encouraged to take cases pro bono where the client cannot afford to pay.

Efforts are now being made to eliminate some unnecessary Law French and Latin terms from the legal vocabulary. The English courts have recently adopted new procedural rules in which the following substitutions were made: *claimant* (instead of plaintiff), *statement of case* (for pleadings), and *disclosure* (replacing discovery).

Change in legal vocabulary is possible. It is largely through the efforts of the *plain language* movement that such change has been brought about, and that is the subject of the next section.

PLAIN LEGAL LANGUAGE

The *plain language* movement (sometimes called *plain English*) has its roots in critiques of political and bureaucratic language in the mid-twentieth century. In 1945, Rudolf Flesch described official government language as *officialese* or *gobbledygook*.[8] Flesch went on to devise a test of the understandability of writing based on measures of word and sentence length. At about the same time, the novelist George Orwell (the author of *1984*) criticized political language in reaction to the distortions and excesses of war propaganda. The rules of clear writing that Orwell proposed remain relevant today:

i. Never use a metaphor, simile, or other figure of speech which you are used to seeing in print.

ii. Never use a long word where a short one will do.

iii. If it is possible to cut a word out, always cut it out.

iv. Never use the passive where you can use the active.

v. Never use a foreign phrase, a scientific word or a jargon word if you can think of an everyday English equivalent.

vi. Break any of these rules sooner than say anything outright barbarous.[9]

Ernest Gowers took up the challenge of reforming official language, and in 1948 produced a guide to plain writing for the English government, and the latest edition continues to be used.[10] It was not until the 1970s, however, that the need for plain language in legal speech and writing was widely recognized. In the United States, legislation was passed requiring plain language in some consumer contracts, and the federal government adopted plain language objectives. International organizations dedicated to promoting the use of plain language such as *Clarity International* were formed, and today there is an extensive literature on plain legal language including guides and critiques.

It is not surprising that some lawyers and judges have opposed the move to plain legal language. The principal counter-arguments have been that plain language is not as precise as traditional legal language, and that using new words may create doubt about whether long-accepted meanings based on traditional terminology are still valid. The supporters of plain language reject these objections. They counter that old forms of documents and traditional wording have their faults and should not be perpetuated as if they were perfect; that plain language can be just as precise, and is not intended to change the meaning and intent of the law; and that plain language is more efficient because meanings are clear at first glance.

Legislation is often the target of criticism for its lack of plain language. Traditions of *legislative drafting* (writing legislation) go back to the nineteenth century and follow patterns that are not found today in ordinary speech or documents. For instance, it is a common practice to state all the conditions related to a required or prohibited act before actually indicating what must be done or avoided. Consider this hypothetical rule of the road: "When entering an intersection which is not controlled by traffic signals or signs, and where the intersecting roads are both highways with the same number of lanes, the driver of a vehicle, except an emergency vehicle with its lights flashing, shall yield the right of way to vehicles on their right." This type of composition leaves readers hanging: they have to finish reading the entire section before learning what the law requires. In very long rules of this type, it is sometimes easy to lose sight of all the conditions and exceptions, thus interfering with understanding the section as a whole. In defence of legislative drafters, it has been recognized that they face a difficult question: what is the audience for a statute? Is it lawyers, judges, the general public, or just those members of the public who will be directly affected by the law? The target audience will probably vary depending on the type of legislation in question, perhaps requiring different styles of drafting to meet the needs of the expected audience in each case.

Using plain language is also recommended in legal speech. There are many instances where the public is orally addressed for legal purposes by judges, lawyers, and police. Unless what is said is correctly understood, justice may not be done. Where there is a criminal trial with a jury, the judge gives instructions to the jury about the law and their duty to consider all the evidence. If this oral presentation is not clearly understood, the verdict may be faulty. Police give *cautions* to those they arrest concerning their right to remain silent under the law and also advise them of their rights to hire a lawyer. If these statements are not well understood, an arrested person may give up their rights in error. These are situations where the liberty of a person may depend upon the clearness or incomprehensibility of oral legal language.

Richard Darville and Gayla Reid provide some plain language guidelines:

- Say who does what to whom (avoid passive constructions like "the form must be filed . . . ")
- Write sentences that flow forward (avoid interrupting sentences with too many subclauses)
- Replace "difficult" words with familiar ones (use "get" instead of "acquire"; "end" instead of "expiry")
- Explain technical words and *terms of art* (ordinary words that have a special legal meaning)[11]

Here are some examples Darville and Reid give of terms of art and their plain language counterparts: *action* (legal proceeding); the *Bar* (lawyers); the *Bench* (judges); *damages* (compensation); *find* a fact or *hold* a correct interpretation (decide something, when done by a judge).[12]

Is it possible, using plain language, to make all legal writing and speech perfectly understandable to the average member of the public? There are arguments for and against this proposition. Perhaps legal language is so embedded in the thinking, writing, and speaking of professionals within the legal system that it must inevitably remain somewhat foreign and incomprehensible to average members of the public. Wider-spread legal literacy may help to counteract this tendency by making the public more familiar with legal language which will hopefully then become more understandable. It should not be necessary to become a lawyer in order to be able to work effectively with legal language.

Plain legal language is also important in *contracts*, where the involved parties need to know their rights and obligations under the agreement. Plain language critics have criticized many large businesses such as banks and insurance companies for using contracts with wording that is complex, archaic, and sometimes printed so small as to be almost illegible—the infamous "fine print." One response has been government action either to prescribe clearer wording by law that businesses must use in their documents or to require that some contracts be reviewed for clarity before being approved for use. Today, many companies make it part of their marketing strategy to proclaim that their documents are in plain language and thus consumer-friendly.

A noted Canadian scholar of legislation and legal interpretation, Ruth Sullivan, has considered whether laws can be made understandable for all. In her view, no single approach to legislative drafting will be satisfactory. Rather, "a commitment to direct and effective communication entails constant experiment and change in the service of maximum personalization."[13] "Personalization" for Sullivan means that the most vulnerable members of the public affected by statutes (who may not be able to afford a lawyer to interpret it for them) should be helped by the wording of the text to understand how the law affects them. Improved legal literacy among the public would also help to achieve this worthy goal. We will examine again the limits of using plain language in law in Chapter 8 when considering legal interpretation.

LANGUAGE RIGHTS

Most people think it is important to be able to read the law, and to be allowed to speak and write in legal proceedings in a language they feel comfortable with. If they are unable to do this, a legal system may lose legitimacy in their eyes. For this reason, *language rights* are part of the law in many countries, particularly those where two or more languages are spoken by large numbers of citizens. Canada is a prime example. Language rights are included in several sections of the Charter of Rights and Freedoms. Section 16(1) states that Canada has two official languages, English and French, and Section 19(1) states that both languages may be used in all federally created courts.. This protection applies to provincial courts, with judges appointed in this way. Section 14 of the Charter gives the right to have an interpreter to anyone who does not understand the language of legal proceedings. According to section 18, statutes passed by Parliament must be published in the two official languages, and both versions are equally authoritative. Constitutionally protected language rights can have real effect, as shown by the decision of the Supreme Court of Canada in the case *Re. Manitoba Language Rights*.[14] The court decided that many provincial statutes were invalid because they were not published in French, but allowed the government time to have them translated, and thus kept on the books.

Some groups of Canadians think further language rights should be established. In 2009, the government of the Territory of Nunavut passed a law giving greater recognition to the language of the Inuit people. Language groups in other countries also seek greater legal rights. For instance, Scotland has secured the right for its ministers to interact with the European Union in Scots Gaelic.

Writing legislation so that it is easily understood is difficult enough when using one language, but it is even more challenging with two because both languages may not have corresponding words for some legal concepts. The French language, for instance, has been used in the Civil Code of France and Québec, but this system has concepts that are not duplicated in the common law. And the converse is also true for common law concepts normally expressed in English that are not found in the legal language of civil code systems. The problem is made even more difficult in Canada by the requirement that both language versions are considered equally authoritative; the meaning in one language does not prevail over a different meaning in the other. How can you express the same meaning in two languages with divergent concepts? Roderick A. MacDonald calls this the problem of *legal bilingualism*. He emphasizes the point that mere translation is not enough. That approach, he suggests, leads to bureaucratic language being adopted merely because it is easy to translate, but which does not express the legal meaning accurately. MacDonald advocates full bilingualism in legal practice: "Legal bilingualism would ultimately require bilingualism in all its practitioners. Rather than encouraging or even allowing two distinct official legal cultures to form around two languages, the practice of legal bilingualism would draw on both languages to construct one official legal culture."[15]

Much progress toward such a goal has been made in writing statutes in Canada. The current legislative drafting practice in the federal government includes paired, co-equal drafters in both official languages, use of *jurilin-guists* (linguistic experts specialized in legal language), and drafting guidelines tailored to both languages.

Canada is not the only country that must deal with the problem of expressing law in two (or more) languages. For example, in Hong Kong the legal system is based on common law traditions reflecting its former status as a British domain. However, the law is now expressed in Mandarin, the language used in mainland China for current legislation in the civil code tradition. Legislative drafters in Hong Kong face many of the same challenges as their Canadian counterparts. It may, however, be an advantage to be required to look at law through the lenses of two languages. Making law in two languages can contribute to enriching its expression and stimulating its development in both languages.

CRITICAL PERSPECTIVES ON LEGAL LANGUAGE

Criticism of the way lawyers and judges speak and write is not new. In the nineteenth century, the English legal reformer Jeremy Bentham called it "law jargon," "lawyers' cant," and "flash language."[16] Great improvements have been made since then. A document commonly used by courts in Alberta formerly read as follows:

ELIZABETH THE SECOND, BY THE GRACE OF GOD OF THE UNITED KINGDOM, CANADA AND HER OTHER REALMS AND TERRITORIES, QUEEN, HEAD OF THE COMMONWEALTH, DEFENDER OF THE FAITH.

TO. . . .

NOW KNOW YE that We, in confidence of your prudence and fidelity, have appointed and do by this Commission appoint you, and direct, authorize and give you power within thirty days after the receipt of this Commission, or such longer time as may reasonably be required to take evidence in the above cause, to examine before you viva voce as herein mentioned the aforesaid witnesses. . . . [17]

This document appoints someone to record and report the evidence of a witness who is outside the territorial jurisdiction of the court, but the language and composition are archaic, and the meaning is not obvious at first reading. Under the revised *Alberta Rules of Court* that came into effect in 2010, this form of appointment now reads:

Order that evidence be taken outside Alberta

The Court is convinced that it is necessary to question [name] ("the Witness") in the jurisdiction in which the witness resides and therefore orders as follows:

1. The evidence of the Witness is authorized to be taken before [name] ("the Examiner").
2. The Examiner must follow these instructions:

   (a) a transcript of the evidence must be prepared;
   (b) evidence must be taken under oath . . .

3. The Witness must produce the following records. . . .[18]

Another court form currently used in Alberta is quite straightforward in its language:

Notice to the third party defendant(s)

You only have a short time to do something to respond to this third party claim:

20 days if you are served in Alberta

1 month if you are served outside Alberta but in Canada
2 months if you are served outside Canada.

You can respond by filing a statement of defence or a demand for notice in the office of the clerk of the Court of Queen's Bench at _____, Alberta, AND serving your statement of defence or a demand for notice on the defendant's(s') /third party plaintiff's(s') address for service.

WARNING

If you do not file and serve a statement of defence or a demand for notice within your time period, you risk losing the claim against you automatically. If you do not file, or do not serve or are late in doing either of these things, a court may give judgment to the defendant(s)/third party plaintiff(s) against you.[19]

This document is a notice to someone (called a *Third Party*) who is being added to an existing legal action because the defendant has a related claim against them. This addition allows the court to deal with all aspects of a legal dispute involving several parties at one time.

However, even this recently revised document contains phrases that may not be easily understood, such as *address for service* (place to which notices may be sent), and *demand for notice* (request to be notified). If a defendant is someone who has been sued, why are they referred to as "defendant's(s')/third party plaintiff's(s')"? It seems legal language is still out of the ordinary. Why is it so resistant to change?

One way to answer this question is by taking into account the different audiences to which laws may be addressed. Is it intended to be read by a member of the public, a judge, or other official? In defence of legal language, it has been said that so long as the public understands it when necessary, then it can continue to take the form of legalese for lawyers and judges because it causes no problems for them. This apology for uncommon legal language holds less weight when you recall that in a modern democracy, law is supposed to represent the will of the people, and lawyers are expected to serve the public. Another response to the problem of legal language suggests that it does change, but much more slowly than society. According to this view, new social ideas and practices must first become sufficiently widespread and well accepted before becoming capable of influencing the concepts and language of law.

Some criticize the use of legalese because its primary purpose seems to be to maintain lawyers' status as elite professionals. Perhaps it is a way of mystifying the law so that the public is forced to rely on lawyers to "translate" for them. This is a conspiracy theory about the problem of legal language. It is more probable that many of the traditions and practices of the legal system, such as legal education, act to socialize lawyers into a professional culture that simply takes for granted the existence of a unique language and discourse.

Let's look more closely at how the language of lawyers and judges differs from ordinary speech and writing. David Mellinkoff lists some notable idiosyncrasies of legal language:

- use of common words with uncommon meanings (e.g., *commission*, meaning a formal appointment in writing)
- use of old, rare, and foreign words (e.g., *viva voce*, meaning orally in person)
- use of terms of art (e.g. *examine*, meaning question)
- use of formal words (e.g. We)
- use of words with flexible meanings (e.g., reasonably)
- use of words to be extremely precise (e.g., within thirty days)
- use of redundant words (e.g., appoint, direct, authorize, and [em] power)[20]

Mellinkoff describes the overall style of legal language as unclear, pompous, and dull! He also lists the common justifications given by lawyers for maintaining it: greater precision, and shorter, more intelligible, more durable documents. In conclusion, Mellinkoff suggests that these desirable goals do not always require the *status quo* to be retained. Improvement in legal language is possible without sacrificing its value within the legal system.

The worst excesses of legalese are found in documents that record transactions such as contracts, wills, and leases, according to Peter M. Tiersma. These texts are *operative* in the sense that they perform legal actions such as selling, leasing, or giving property on death. Tiersma suggests that because they must be taken seriously by the people who sign them, and stand up to challenges by the other party, these documents must be wordy and follow recognized forms. Nevertheless he acknowledges "it is highly ironic that documents with the most legalese (like contracts, wills, deeds, and statutes) are also most likely to be read by clients and directly affect their interests."[21]

The most serious question that arises from the uniqueness of legal language is whether it is a case of "the law versus the people."[22] Is legal language a barrier that restricts the public from using and benefiting from law? The plain language movement seems to be narrowing the gap between ordinary and legal language, but so long as the legal system maintains its position of relative autonomy from the rest of society, legal discourse and legal language will remain a challenge for people seeking justice through law.

CHAPTER REVIEW

After reading this chapter you should be able to:

- list some characteristics of legal language that have been criticized
- describe some features of legal discourse
- explain the history of legal vocabulary
- explain the concept of plain legal language
- list some improvements in legal language that can make it more understandable
- give some examples of language rights

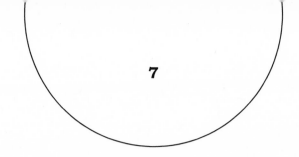

LEGAL RESEARCH

Skills and Techniques for Researching Law

Generic research skills used in any discipline may be sufficient to begin an initial legal analysis and investigate legal processes and procedures at the start of a case. Another person may have started legal action, and their documents may provide some research and analysis that can be built on. For example, an individual can access an online legal dictionary to look up the legal references and words they have used. He or she can study legal procedures by downloading the rules of court from a court's website. As a legal matter progresses, however, it becomes important to be able to do more complex research to improve the strength of a claim and to raise doubts about that of the other side. Arguments based on law require competent legal research to be credible in the eyes of a judge or tribunal.

The goal of legal research is to find laws or precedents that support your arguments and undermine those of the other side. This is a search for *authorities* (precedents and other authoritative statements of law) that may be presented to a decision-maker to support a legal argument. When a judge asks, "what is the authority for that statement?" the results of prior legal research help to provide a credible and persuasive response. The legal system is capable of change, but it is much easier to convince a judge to follow existing legal authorities than to break with long-standing interpretations of the law and established precedents. In exceptional cases it may be possible to find a section of the Constitution, or a decision of the highest court in the jurisdiction that can be presented to a judge as a *binding authority* that makes any counter-argument virtually impossible. Such a case would likely be settled without the necessity of a trial (if the facts were not in doubt) once both sides of the dispute became aware of such authority. Many legal matters, however, are not so cut-and-dried, and research is usually necessary to find helpful authorities that may come from all levels of the legal hierarchy, including local legislation and decisions from lower courts.

Before the existence of the Internet, legal research was conducted in law libraries found in courthouses, law schools, and private legal firms. Law librarians over many hundreds of years adopted unique conventions for cataloguing and displaying legal materials that law students learned about as part of their training in conducting research. The distinctive organization of law libraries to some extent physically mirrored the structures and hierarchies of law itself. Legislation and legal decisions were contained in books shelved chronologically and located in separate sections, each dedicated to a single legal jurisdiction; textbooks, reference works, and journal articles were housed in their own areas—this structured arrangement of materials helped to focus legal research, making it more efficient and effective. The print era of legal research, however, is now largely over and huge quantities of legal materials are now available in digital format, often free of charge on the web. This has had the effect of opening up more avenues of legal research, but it has also magnified the problem of identifying which legal authorities will be accepted and used by a decision-maker in a particular case.

This chapter examines the purposes of legal research, the tools and techniques that are available to do it, and some obstacles that get in the way of doing it well. Today, finding legal materials is much easier than when it was necessary to visit a law library, but evaluating the results of online searches—determining the value of what you find as legal authority—is a new challenge for researchers whether legal professionals or not.

Individuals may research the law and legal system for a variety of reasons in addition to making or responding to a legal claim. The field defines different approaches to legal research according to the perspective and corresponding objective of the researcher. An internal perspective regarding legal research accepts the existing framework of the law, the legal system, its processes and procedures, and seeks the results of research for the purpose of practical use. Lawyers typically have an internal perspective when they do legal research for their clients. An external perspective does not accept the inevitability of existing law and legal systems, and seeks legal knowledge for the purpose of advancing a critique of them. Academics, such as law professors and scholars of legal studies, often adopt an external perspective when they do research for the purpose of law reform. From an internal perspective, the purpose of doing legal research is to obtain a desired result using legal processes. From an external perspective, the purpose of research is to understand the relations between law and society, and generate ideas about how law might better serve it.

Research done by lawyers from an internal perspective is called doctrinal legal research. Its purpose is to discover the doctrines (legal principles and rules) that can be used to persuade a judge to decide in a client's favour. Legal academics also do this type of research to contribute to the better understanding of existing law, and sometimes with a view to developing it in new directions. Because doctrinal research is primarily concerned with analyzing legal texts (legislation and case reports) it is sometimes described as the study of black-letter law (law as written rules).

The results of doctrinal legal research appear in the written submissions (written arguments, called briefs in the United States) that lawyers present to judges. When done by legal scholars, doctrinal research appears in periodicals called law journals (or law reviews). Another type of research done from an internal perspective is theoretical inquiry about the nature and status of law, called jurisprudence (or legal philosophy). Note that the word jurisprudence is sometimes also used in a different way when talking about the law. In this alternative meaning, it is used to describe the legal principles and interpretations established in precedent cases. This other meaning of jurisprudence is used to contrast that part of the law with legislation.

Legal research from an external perspective may be done with the addition of concepts and research methods from other scholarly disciplines, and therefore has a variety of names. Some areas of research and study are sociology of law, economics and law, law and psychology, socio-legal research (also known as law in context and law and society), law reform and legal studies research. The results of these types of research sometimes appear in law journals, but more often in interdisciplinary publications and the scholarly journals of fields such as sociology and psychology. Law reform research often results in a discussion paper or report that is published by the reform agency for consideration by lawmakers who may wish to change or amend the law.

A study of legal research has classified all of the many types on a grid. One axis of description extends from doctrinal at one end to interdisciplinary at the other. The other axis features pure research (seeking knowledge for its own sake) and applied research (gaining knowledge for practical use) at its poles.[1] In Australia, legal research has been described in broad terms:

> Legal research today may be thought to be considerably broader than
> the tripartite classification [doctrinal, reform-oriented and theoretical], as
> it embraces empirical research (resonating with the social sciences), his-
> torical research (resonating with the humanities), comparative research
> (permeating all categories), research into the institutions and processes
> of the law, and interdisciplinary research (especially, though by no
> means exclusively, research into law and society).[2]

Terry Hutchinson suggests that today's lawyers need more than the bibliographic skills (skills in finding written information) which are most often used in doctrinal legal research.[3] In Hutchinson's view, the qualitative and quantitative research methods common in other disciplines should also be part of a lawyer's skill set. The field of legal studies already embraces such interdisciplinary methods in the study of law.

This book reflects both an internal and an external perspective on the law. From the internal perspective, it presents information useful for working within the legal system to achieve goals. Thus, in this chapter, I go on to describe traditional methods of doctrinal legal research used by the legal profession, many of which can also be used effectively by non-lawyers. The concluding section of the chapter, like similar sections throughout this book, presents critical ideas based on research and study that has been done primarily from an external perspective on the legal system.

Some readers may be tempted to skip this section because they never expect to enter a law library. That would be a mistake for at least three good reasons:

1. becoming familiar with the organization and arrangement of law libraries yields insight into the structure of law, which contributes to more effective legal planning and research whether done in print or online;

2. some valuable legal materials are not easily accessible online, but can be found on the shelves of law libraries;

3. many law libraries have websites that include useful guides to finding online legal materials.

Publicly accessible law libraries are found in three locations: university law schools, courthouses, and legislatures (or associated government buildings). Most general public libraries have only small collections of legal materials. Law libraries are organized differently from other libraries. The items on the shelves are not arranged either by using Dewey Decimal call numbers (numbers 340 to 349.9) or by Library of Congress alphabetical classification (class K). Instead, law libraries organize their collections according to the source of law found in different types of publication. In common law systems there are two principal *sources of law*: statutes (legislation), and reports of judicial decisions (precedents). Statutes are always published separately from case reports, and therefore these two types of materials are shelved in different locations in law libraries.

There is slightly different terminology used to refer to the decisions of judges depending upon the jurisdiction. In Canada and the United Kingdom, such decisions are usually called *judgments* (note the spelling). In the United States they are called *opinions*. These contain judges' justifications for their decisions, explaining how they followed (and sometimes interpreted) the law and decided the facts. The formal document that records the result of the decision (which party is to be paid, for instance) is often called an *order* of the court, although sometimes it is called a *formal judgment*. When a judge writes a judgment or opinion, it may be published in print or online as a case report found in a series of volumes known as a *reporter*, or *report series*.

Law libraries have a section devoted entirely to statutes, within which the materials will be organized by territorial jurisdiction. Therefore, in a Canadian law library you will find a section containing all federal legislation and there will be sections for each of the provinces and territories, perhaps in alphabetical order. The statutes of each jurisdiction will be shelved in date order, according to when they were passed by the legislators, going back in time to the founding of the country, or even further to the colonial period. At some points on these many shelves containing legislation are volumes labelled *revised statutes*. These are periodic collections of all the statutes in a jurisdiction that have not been *repealed* (declared to be no longer law), with all *amendments* (changes or additions) made since the legislation was first passed incorporated into the text. *Consolidated statutes* are much the same thing, but are produced for individual statutes more often than revisions of all legislation. The most recent legislation to have been passed may be in unbound printed form (*loose parts*) and will be published in an annual volume at a later date. The *Queen's Printer* (official government publisher) for British Columbia provides a useful online glossary of terms used in connection with legislation.[4]

Case reports are also found together in a separate section in a law library. They are usually organized by geographical jurisdiction, and may be further subdivided (into national and provincial jurisdictions, for instance). Some series of case reports are dedicated to specific subject matter jurisdictions such as tax, criminal law, and family law. The volumes of reports within a jurisdiction are shelved by date according to when the decisions were made and published, and may be subdivided into series (volumes consecutively numbered covering a certain span of years). An example of this is the *Dominion Law Reports* containing decisions from across Canada. As of 2009, these reports were in their fourth series of volumes that began in 1984. Before that, date volumes belonged to the third series of these reports.

Another important section of a law library is the collection of law journals (reviews) containing scholarly articles, usually arranged alphabetically by journal title and shelved by publication date. Law libraries also have a separate section for *legal treatises* (scholarly texts, or monographs) dealing with specific legal subjects (like criminal law, or wills and estates). These volumes may be shelved according to the Dewey Decimal or Library of Congress scheme. In common law systems, judges may occasionally refer to these scholarly publications for guidance in deciding cases, and therefore they represent another potential source of law when accepted by courts as being correct.

Law libraries will also have a reference section containing publications such as *law dictionaries*, *legal encyclopedias*, and *legal digests* (brief summaries of cases indexed according to the legal issues discussed in the decisions). Legal reference works may also be found online, but usually only through publishers' websites that are restricted to subscribed customers. To make use of these valuable legal research tools, you may therefore have to visit a law library.

Many law libraries have embraced the open access principle, and have made valuable research materials available on or through their websites. Here is a list of some Canadian courthouse (or Law Society) library websites providing valuable public access to legal research materials online and some research guidance:

Alberta	www.lawlibrary.ab.ca/
British Columbia	www.courthouselibrary.ca/
Manitoba	www.lawsociety.mb.ca/manitoba-law-libraries/
New Brunswick	www.nblawlib-bib.ca/
Newfoundland & Labrador	www.lslibrary.ca/
Nova Scotia	http://nsbs.org/library_services
Ontario	www.lsuc.on.ca/greatlibrary.aspx
Prince Edward Island	www.lspei.pe.ca/law_library.php
Saskatchewan	www.lawsociety.sk.ca/newlook/Library/library.htm
Northwest Territories	www.justice.gov.nt.ca/dbtw-wpd/nwtjqbe.shtml
Nunavut	www.nucj.ca/library/library.htm
Yukon	www.justice.gov.yk.ca/prog/cs/library.html

LEGAL CITATION

The term *legal citation*, like many words in law, has several related but distinct meanings depending on the context in which they are used. One of the primary meanings of the verb *to cite* is to refer to and possibly quote from something; this is similar to the meaning intended when someone *cites a case* as a precedent. In law this is called *citing from authority*—referring to, and perhaps quoting from, a case or a statute that is an authoritative statement of the law. Therefore, in this setting legal citation means the process of using precedent (or legislation) to support an argument. In the same context, we find the term *citator* referring to a publication containing an index of cases or statutes. A *case citator* contains cross references of decisions that have been cited in subsequent cases either as precedents or in other ways. Such an index is one way of finding out if a judgment has been appealed or if it has been considered by judges in other jurisdictions. The index in a *statute citator* allows you to trace the history of legislation (amendments and repeals), and to find reported cases that consider and interpret particular statutes.

A related meaning of the term legal citation is the way in which cases or statutes are referenced when they are cited. In this context, a *system of legal citation* is an approved or preferred style of referencing, like those used in other disciplines. Thus, if a judge asked "What is the citation for that case?" he or she wants the reference data in the accepted legal format (the *case citation*). Sometimes *cite* is used as a noun in place of the full word citation in that context ("here's the cite for the case you asked for").

Finally, it should be noted that there is yet another legal use of the term *citation* based on an alternative meaning of the verb "to cite," which is "to summon." Thus, if you are *cited for contempt* it means you are being summoned to appear before a judge to explain your actions. Such an order is contained in a document known as a *contempt citation*.

Systems of accepted legal citation vary by jurisdiction. In Canada, one of the most commonly accepted is that used by the *McGill Law Journal* when publishing articles. In the United States it is the *Bluebook* system promoted by Harvard Law School that is most widely accepted. A unique feature of most systems of legal citation is that they usually begin with a year or volume number, rather than the name of the publication. This reflects the legal system's concern for the currency of legal sources—the most recent case (or the appeal decision in a case), and the current version of legislation containing all amendments are usually the best authorities.

In the past, most case reports were provided by private publishers, such as the *Dominion Law Reports* in Canada issued by the Carswell Company, or the *National Reporters* issued by West Publishing Company in the United States. Therefore, access to those volumes was necessary in order to cite a case and provide its citation in court. This necessity supported a strong commercial demand for these publications, and these created successful private monopolies based on access to sources of law. As part of the movement for open access to law, it was recommended that courts provide *neutral citations* for their judgments. A neutral citation is not tied to the page numbers in a privately published case report series, and therefore allows cases to be cited without requiring access to commercial publications. Neutral citations typically consist of the year the decision was made, the name of the court issuing it, and a consecutive number assigned by the court to the decision. To assist with citing specific parts of judgments, many courts have also adopted the practice of numbering the paragraphs in their decisions. This allows lawyers to give an exact citation for a quotation from a judgment that is not tied to page numbers in a printed volume. Of course, it is necessary to first read the case to be cited, and courts have assisted with the publication of judgments in addition to their citation.

Let's examine the legal citation of a case in detail, taking as an example an important case in Canadian copyright law we will examine later in this chapter. As with all referencing systems, the primary purpose of legal citation is to allow the source of a document to be located and the original examined if so desired. How does legal citation do this?

Here is the neutral citation for the case:

CCH Canadian Ltd. v. Law Society of Upper Canada, 2004 SCC 13

This citation tells us that the case was decided in 2004, but it is not immediately obvious by which court. Legal citations usually use abbreviations for the names of courts and publications. You might guess that "scc" stands for Supreme Court of Canada (and you would be right), but you can check using an index of legal abbreviations. The citation also informs us that the decision was the thirteenth issued by the court in that year, but does not help us to locate it. Later in this chapter, I will provide guidance on locating legal materials for reading.

Here is a *parallel citation* (citation containing two or more references) for the same case. A parallel citation includes information about alternative sources in which the case report may be found.

CCH Canadian Ltd. v. Law Society of Upper Canada, 2004 SCC 13, [2004] 1 S.C.R., 339

This citation includes the further information that a report of the case may be found in a volume containing cases decided in 2004 in a publication abbreviated as "S.C.R." Looking up that abbreviation, we find that it stands for *Supreme Court Reports*, the official printed versions of decisions of the Supreme Court of Canada. The "1" indicates that there were several volumes of cases from 2004, and we must look in the first of them. The page number is at the end. This citation allows us to locate and read the case report if we can find a library with this publication on its shelves. We would look for volumes labelled *Supreme Court Reports*, go to those for the year 2004, choose the first volume of that year, and find page 339.

Here is a further parallel citation providing even more publications in which one can find this important case:

CCH Canadian Ltd. v. Law Society of Upper Canada, 2004 SCC 13, [2004] 1 S.C.R. 339, 236 D.L.R. (4th) 395, 30 C.P.R. (4th) 1, 247 F.T.R. 318

Finally, here is a citation for the same case in a format that is used in a particular commercial legal database (LawSource):

2004 CarswellNat 446

This is a citation in a private format adopted by Westlaw Canada, allowing a report of the case to be retrieved through the LawSource online commercial database. Such a citation would not be acceptable in court.

Statutes and *regulations* (subsidiary laws made under authority of a statute) are also cited according to an accepted system of citation. Here is an example for a law we will discuss later in the chapter:

Reproduction of Federal Law Order S.I./97-5, C.Gaz. 1997. II. 444

Using an abbreviation index, we can discover that the citation refers to a *statutory instrument* (S.I.—a document having the force of law, but not contained in a statute or regulation) made in 1997 and published in the *Canadian Gazette* (C.Gaz., a government publication), part II, at page 444. These abbreviations are explained in a glossary of legislative terms provided online by the Canadian Government.[5]

Here is a citation for a federal statute:

Copyright Act, R.S.C. 1985, c. C-42

In most jurisdictions, governments have retained responsibility for publishing legislation and have not put it in the hands of private firms. For Commonwealth countries, the official government publisher is usually known as the *Queen's Printer*. Accordingly, citations to statutes assume that the official version as published by the government is being cited. Recently, the Canadian government and others, have made the online versions of legislation official. This means that the version found on the Internet is considered to be the authoritative statement of the law, instead of that found in print.

Using abbreviation indexes, we can discover that the *Copyright Act* referred to above is found in the Revised Statutes of Canada (R.S.C.), revised as of 1985, at the *chapter* (c.) labelled C-42 (the 42nd statute under "C" in alphabetical order). The use of the term "chapter" indicates that all the legislation in a particular jurisdiction is considered to form one large figurative "book" (the *statute book*) and that separate *Acts* (pieces of legislation) on different topics are the individual chapters of it.

Here is an example of citation of a Canadian provincial statute:

Queen's Printer Act, R.S.A. 2000, c. Q-2

This citation follows the same format as the federal *Copyright Act*. This provincial legislation may be found in the volumes of the *Revised Statutes of Alberta* (R.S.A.) as of the year 2000 at chapter Q-2. However, not all legislation is contained in revised statutes. Here is an example of a citation of legislation that is not:

Civil Marriage Act, S.C. 2005, c. 33

The *Civil Marriage Act* may be found in a collection of the *Statutes of Canada* (S.C.) passed by Parliament in 2005; it was the thirty-third piece of legislation enacted that year. This act will eventually be incorporated in future set of revised statutes, and will be given a new chapter number when that is done.

LEGAL RESEARCH STRATEGY

There is no single best way of doing legal research. Research experts have emphasized that it should be approached as a strategy, and cannot be conducted by simply following a checklist or standard format every time.

As I already mentioned, doctrinal legal research has traditionally meant a search for an authority that can support arguments in a case. In common law legal systems, this means textual authority found in legislation or case precedents (and sometimes treatises). Computerized and online searches give people the ability to look for texts that mention the same legal issues or describe a factual situation similar to their case. The goal is to find the section of a statute or decision of a judge that supports the argument they wish to make. Word-matching, however, is not a sound strategy for good legal research. It often results in a mass of disorganized material, and the problem of not being able "to see the forest for the trees" or mistaking the value of what is found. Non-lawyers are particularly disadvantaged by such excess information because they have no internalized conceptual map of the law and its processes to guide them in evaluating search results.

What alternative strategies are there for legal research? Again, experts have pointed to the need for the researcher to first assemble a context within which to evaluate the legal sources they find. The goal is to create a mental map of the wider "neighbourhood" of law in question before becoming lost in the twists and turns of particular cases, rules, or principles that are discovered through intensive research. Another way of putting it is to consider generalities first before proceeding with a detailed analysis of particulars. Such a strategy helps the researcher avoid two serious errors: citing a decision in a case that was appealed, resulting in the decision being reversed and making it worthless as precedent; citing a statute that was amended or repealed, thus negating its value as legislation to be followed.

Here are some important criteria for evaluating and selecting *primary legal materials* (legislation or reported cases) as authorities to support a legal argument.

Assuming that the individual has found a case with similar facts to the one being argued, the criteria for evaluating it as a persuasive case authority are: the case should be from a court in the jurisdiction of the dispute; the higher the level of the court in that jurisdiction, the better; the more recent the case, the better; the more times the case has been cited with approval in other cases, the better; the case must not have been successfully appealed and the decision reversed.

For legislation (including statutes, regulations, rules, and bylaws) important criteria for evaluation are: the legislation must be from the jurisdiction of the dispute and be in force; if there is a choice, statutes are better than regulations, rules, or bylaws; regulations, rules, or bylaws must not be contrary to the statute; a constitution is the highest authority and everything else must be constitutional (that is, not contradict the constitution); the legislation must not have been repealed or amended.

It is sometimes necessary or desirable, however, to research the state of the law as it existed in the past, even though it is no longer in effect. This may be done as part of historical or law reform research, or because a statute was changed after the events in question in a particular dispute. The legal principle that law should normally not have *retroactive effect* means that past events are governed by the law in force at that time, not the law as it stands today if it has since changed. Therefore, research must reveal the state of the law at some earlier date. Some online legislative databases now offer *point in time searching* to facilitate such historical research.

Important legal concepts and ideas will be mentioned in several statutes, many cases, treatises, and scholarly articles. The strategic goal of *contextual legal research* is to sample all of those sources without going too deeply into them at first. Comparing the treatment of a legal concept, rule, or principle across multiple legal materials helps to bring out the conceptual structure of the law in the area. Once the researcher grasps that overall structure, it will then be useful and informative to look closely at individual cases or the details of legislation.

A legal research strategy in a particular situation will be guided by the information available to begin with. This may be the name of a case, the section number of an act, regulation, or bylaw, or words describing a legal problem or public issue. I have provided below some strategies appropriate to each of those starting points.

First, how can a researcher progress from reading a particular case to understanding the wider legal context in which the decision was rendered? The text of a case itself often provides an introduction to the context surrounding it. Here are some excerpts from the report of the CCH case cited above as an example:

Copyright—Infringement—Exception—Fair dealings—Law Society providing custom photocopy service and maintaining self-service photocopiers in library for use by patrons—Legal publishers bringing copyright infringement actions against Law Society—Whether Law Society's dealings with publishers' works fair dealings. *Copyright Act*, R.S.C. 1985, c. C-42, s. 29.

Cases Cited

Applied: *Muzak Corp. v. Composers, Authors and Publishers Association of Canada, Ltd.*, [1953] 2 S.C.R. 182; *De Tervagne v. Belœil* (Town), [1993] 3 F.C. 227; not followed: *Moorhouse v. University of New South Wales*, [1976] R.P.C. 151; referred to: Moreau v. St. Vincent, [1950] Ex. C.R. 198; . . .

Statutes and Regulations Cited

Berne Convention for the Protection of Literary and Artistic Works (1886).
Copyright Act, R.S.C. 1985, c. C-42, ss. 2 "computer program" [am. c. 10 (4th Supp.), s. 1(3)], "dramatic work" [am. 1993, c. 44, s. 53(2)], "every original literary, dramatic, musical and artistic work" [*idem*], "library, archive or museum" [ad. 1997, c. 24, s. 1(5)] . . .

Authors Cited

Concise Oxford Dictionary of Current English, 7th ed., s.v. "original." Oxford: Oxford University Press, 1982.
Craig, Carys J. "Locke, Labour and Limiting the Author's Right: A Warning against a Lockean Approach to Copyright Law," *Queen's L.J.* 28 (2002), 1.

The *catchwords* (or *keywords*) appearing at the beginning of a case report can be used as signposts—relevant legal terms to use when continuing to research in encyclopedias, treatises, and journal articles, thus building up a picture of the law in the area. The cases cited can lead to other decisions that may mention more key terms, and the statutes cited establish the legislative context.

As a strategy for reading cases, the first step should be to look at more descriptive materials about the relevant area of law, such as legal encyclopedias, to help establish the legal framework for the decision, and only when that has been done should the judgment be read closely. It is easy to get lost reading the details of a decision without first understanding the wider legal context in which it exists. References in the case report to scholarly articles or treatises ("authors cited") lead to explanations and discussions of the legal concepts and principles involved in the case. It is also necessary early on to find out if the decision to be read has been appealed or considered (commented on) in subsequent cases. Since the CCH judgment is from the Supreme Court of Canada, no further appeal is possible, but it may have been discussed in other, later decisions that can also provide insight. A case citator is the place to look for that information.

If the starting point of legal research is a section of legislation, then its context can be discovered using a statute citator or digest. A lawyer in the Canadian Department of Justice has created one such research tool online for the Charter of Rights and Freedoms. It is a citator and digest for decisions in which the Charter has been applied or considered. Here is an excerpt from the entry for Section 2(a) of the Charter that discusses the fundamental freedoms of conscience and religion:

> To state that any legislation which has an effect on religion, no matter how minimal, violates the religious guarantee "would radically restrict the operating latitude of the legislature" (*Braunfeld v. Brown*, 366 U.S. 599). It is arguable that under our Constitution this kind of concern should be dealt with under s.1, but as Wilson, J. stated in Operation Dismantle, "the rights under the Charter not being absolute, their content or scope must be discerned quite apart from any limitation sought to be imposed upon them by the government under s.1." Not every effect of legislation on religious beliefs or practices is offensive to the constitutional guarantee. Section 2(a) does not require the legislature to refrain from imposing any burdens on the practice of religion. Legislative or administrative action whose effect on religion is trivial or insubstantial is not a breach of freedom of religion. This conclusion necessarily follows from the adoption of an effects-based approach to the Charter: *Jones v. R.*, 1986 CanLII 32 (S.C.C.), [1986] 2 S.C.R. 284.[6]

This digest entry provides legal commentary and references to other cases, both Canadian and American.

Finally, if legal research begins with only a few words that appear to have legal significance, then encyclopedias, treatises, and journal articles will help to form the context. The table of contents from a legal encyclopedia is one place to look for the words of interest, and there are collections of materials arranged by legal subject matter online. Today, legal commentary also can be found online via the blogs (or "blawgs") of lawyers, law teachers, and other legal experts. These may provide valuable discussion that helps to increase understanding of the concepts and issues in a particular area of law. An index of law blogs can be found at the Canadian Law Blogs List.[7]

Having gained a better understanding of the concepts, terminology, and principles of an area of law involved in a legal matter, a researcher can then return to the starting point and read all of the legal materials that he or she has collected carefully in detail. I present some ideas on how to get the most out of reading legal materials in the next chapter on legal interpretation.

LEGAL RESEARCH ONLINE

There are now many freely available online collections of legal materials. These are mainly restricted to case reports and legislation, since individual authors often claim copyright in their commentary and analysis of the law, and will not usually allow it to be accessed without charge. Non-profit bodies, universities, and governments (through Queen's Printers and other departments) are the primary providers of freely accessible online legal materials. In Canada, CanLII, the largest open legal database, is provided by the Federation of Law Societies of Canada and produced by LexUM based at the University of Montréal. The advanced search function on CanLII allows an individual to retrieve as narrow or wide a selection of legal materials as desired.

Here are some of the other valuable functions available on CanLII with examples of the results that can be obtained using the *Copyright Act* and the 2004 *CCH Canadian Ltd. v. Law Society of Upper Canada* case as the starting point:

- Point-in-time source of legislation (historical search). For example, a search using CanLII for the *Copyright Act* will also provide links to older, superseded versions of the act; in this instance, a version that was in force between April and December 2005.

Copyright Act, RSC 1985, c C-42 ℝ

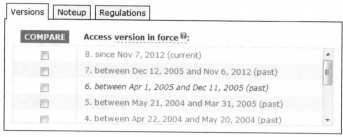

This version is not the latest.

Past version: in force between Apr 1, 2005 and Dec 11, 2005

Link to this version: http://canlii.ca/t/hz9k

Citation to this version: Copyright Act, RSC 1985, c C-42, <http://canlii.ca/t/hz9k>
                             retrieved on 2014-10-07

- Citator for legislation (called *noteup* in CanLII). For example, a search using CanLII for other cases that have considered the *Copyright Act*. These cases are searchable by jurisdiction, venue (court or tribunal in which they were heard), and date.

- Case citator. For example, a search using CanLII for other cases that have considered the CCH case.

All CanLII (91)   **Cases (91)**   Legislation (0)   Commentary (0)

All jurisdictions ▾   All courts and tribunals ▾   Any date ▾   By Relevance ▾   ⌁ in 🐦

1. RTI Turbo inc. c. Canada Allied Diesel Company Ltd., 2007 QCCA 1420 (CanLII) — 2007-10-15
Court of Appeal — Quebec
auteur — originalité — oeuvre — photographié — norme

[...] [5] **2004 CSC 13 (CanLII)**, [2004] 1 R.C.S. 339. [...]

cited by 2 documents

2. Cummings c. Canwest Global Broadcasting Inc., 2007 QCCA 338 (CanLII) — 2007-03-08
Court of Appeal — Quebec
intimées — idée — talent — oeuvre — auteur

[...] V. CCH Canadienne Ltée c. Barreau du Haut-Canada, **2004 CSC 13 (CanLII)**, [2004] 1 R.C.S. 339; [...]

cited by 2 documents

Of course, online legal resources must still be evaluated for their reputability, currency, and accuracy according to the criteria discussed above.

CRITICAL PERSPECTIVE ON LEGAL RESEARCH

It has never been easy to find the law or discover how it works, even for lawyers. Critics have pointed to several reasons for this: the volume of legal materials that keeps growing, control of sources by governments, and control of distribution of materials by publishers.

The law in common law systems has been under development for hundreds of years, beginning in England and now throughout the Commonwealth and the United States. During this time, an enormous amount of written material has accumulated. In many university law school libraries you can find hundreds of thousands of items, and the Law Library of the United States Library of Congress has millions.

A large proportion of legal materials are case reports—the reasons given by judges when deciding individual lawsuits. In early times, only a few of these decisions were recorded and published—this is known as a *selective publishing policy*, and results in a collection of *leading cases* referred to frequently for guidance. In the United States, however, beginning in the nineteenth century one law publisher, West Publishing, decided to publish all decisions of appeal courts. This is known as a *comprehensive publishing policy*. Critics have noted that it results in a mass of cases, most of which are routine and unhelpful to the development of the law. Today, courts find it easy to provide digital versions of judges' decisions and court records online; this amounts to a de facto comprehensive publishing policy. Digitalization of the law has resulted in even more legal materials becoming available, adding to the problem of finding relevant legal information in the mass of online materials.

Another criticism of the field of legal publishing argues that there is actually too little in the way of legal materials publicly available because of government control over sources of legal information. This control is supported by the principle of *Crown copyright*, according to which all materials produced by officials (including judges) belongs to the government, which can therefore prevent or regulate its copying and distribution. The position in the United States is different. There the principle of the *public domain* has been adopted, according to which the public must be given access to all government documents (with some exceptions, such as materials related to national security).

Critics of Crown copyright point out that it is inconsistent with the principle that everyone is presumed to know the law, which cannot operate fairly if the law is not published; that it frustrates democratic scrutiny of law and public participation in law-making[8]; and that legal materials have already been paid for by the public through taxes that pay judges' and officials' salaries.

Governments have recently responded to these criticisms and relaxed control over government documents, particularly legislation and court decisions. One example is the order issued by the federal government in Canada:

Reproduction of Federal Law Order

Whereas it is of fundamental importance to a democratic society that its law be widely known and that its citizens have unimpeded access to that law;

And whereas the Government of Canada wishes to facilitate access to its law by licensing the reproduction of federal law without charge or permission;

Therefore His Excellency the Governor General in Council, on the recommendation of the Minister of Canadian Heritage, the

Minister of Industry, the Minister of Public Works and
Government Services, the Minister of Justice and the Treasury
Board, hereby makes the annexed Reproduction of Federal Law
Order.

Anyone may, without charge or request for permission,
reproduce enactments and consolidations of enactments of the
Government of Canada, and decisions and reasons for decisions
of federally-constituted courts and administrative tribunals,
provided due diligence is exercised in ensuring the accuracy
of the materials reproduced and the reproduction is not
represented as an official version.

S.I./97-5, C.Gaz. 1997. II. 444 (Registration January 8, 1997)

Other governments in Canada, such as the provinces of Ontario and
Alberta, have followed suit.

The movement for *open access* is another response to the problem of restrictions on the distribution of legal materials. Legal academics have been leaders in advocating for and providing open public access to law. The Legal Information Institute at Cornell Law School was one of the first to utilize the Internet for this purpose, followed by the Australasian Legal Information Institute[9] (AustLII), the Canadian Legal Information Institute[10] (CanLII), and others around the world. WorldLII is a federation of such organizations, and has adopted a declaration of open access principles that states,

Public legal information from all countries and international
institutions is part of the common heritage of humanity. Maximising
access to this information promotes justice and the rule of law;

Public legal information is digital common property and should be
accessible to all on a non-profit basis and free of charge;

Organisations such as legal information institutes have the right
to publish public legal information and the government bodies that
create or control that information should provide access to it so that
it can be published by other parties.[11]

A further criticism of the traditional approach to disseminating legal materials is that it should not be under the control of private publishers. In the past, courts often entered into exclusive *licensing agreements* (permission to reproduce copyright materials) with publishers to produce volumes of case reports for sale. The West Publishing Company in the United States gained a virtual monopoly on publishing these essential legal reference works for a century, and similar situations occurred in other countries. Private publishers naturally block the use of their legal publications by those who have not paid for them to protect their commercial interests.

As part of its commercial strategy, West Publishing sought to prevent other publishers from using the page numbers West assigned in their volumes of case reports. Page number references are needed when quoting from the decisions of judges used as precedents, and any publication that lacks them is not suitable for use in court. In the case *Matthew Bender & Co. v. West Publishing Co.*, American courts decided that West could not claim copyright in page numbers.[12] This decision allowed other publishers to produce effective competing products.

In the Canadian case *CCH Canadian Ltd. v. Law Society of Upper Canada*[13] mentioned above, a publisher tried to prevent the Law Society in Ontario from photocopying CCH publications held in in their library to provide copies to lawyers doing legal research. The Canadian courts also decided against the publisher. These cases show that relying on private publishers to provide access to legal materials may not be in the best interests of the legal system and the public. Laws governing the use and distribution of legal materials thus have an important bearing on access to justice. Accordingly, the barriers to legal research is a topic in itself which may be critically investigated by legal studies researchers.

CHAPTER REVIEW

After reading this chapter you should be able to:

- explain the concepts of crown copyright and open access
- describe the different types of legal research

- explain the concepts of legal authority and precedent
- describe the elements of a system of legal citation
- list the principal research tools for finding legislation and court decisions
- find legislation, court decisions and other materials relating to a legal issue

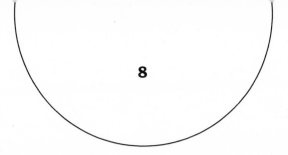

8

LEGAL INTERPRETATION

Skills and Techniques for Making Sense of Law

Legal interpretation is the legal term used to describe the process of reading and giving meaning to law. Legal interpretation is called *legislative interpretation, statutory interpretation*, or sometimes *statutory construction* (from the verb "construe," meaning to analyze or interpret) when it concerns legislation such as acts, regulations, and bylaws. Legal interpretation is also often required when reading private documents such as contracts and wills. In those cases, the generic term is more appropriate. In this chapter, the general term *legal interpretation* will be used throughout.

Unlike a poem, the meaning of which can be left indefinite or ambiguous, differences concerning the interpretation of law must be definitively resolved to allow it to be applied (or not) in a particular case. A judge performs this function, and the resulting judgment may become a precedent for the correct interpretation of a particular section of legislation or the wording of a rule. There are a number of accepted methods and approaches for deciding the proper meaning of laws that are described below. Legal literacy requires a basic understanding of some of these *principles of legal interpretation* that are used to resolve disputes over legal meaning.

When faced with a legal problem, we read judgments for the purpose of selecting those that reflect similar situations and may therefore be used as precedents to guide current decision-making. The careful reading and analysis of reported decisions to discover the principles of law they support is called *legal case analysis*.

Legal interpretation is one of the most complex tools of legal literacy, making it challenging to learn. Here are some of the reasons for the difficulty of legal interpretation:

- Law is stated in general terms because it is normally intended to apply to many people in a variety of situations; however, even general words have limits of meaning, thus requiring interpretation in particular cases.
- In an adversarial legal system, there is an incentive to challenge the meaning of a law if doing so might result in an advantage to a disputing party.
- Law exists within a dense context of interrelated ideas and concepts that allows legal terms to take on different meanings depending on the surrounding wording.
- Many legal terms have two or more different, legally accepted meanings, one of which must be chosen for the purpose of a particular case.

An individual can thus make several types of legal arguments about the proper interpretation of a written law, such as:

- This legislation doesn't apply to me; its *scope* is limited to other people.
- I did not do what is prohibited by this law; my actions were not within the meaning of this rule.
- This law allows for an exception in my case, which is implied in its wording or stated elsewhere.
- I did not intend to harm anyone and therefore should not be found guilty of an offence; *mens rea* is required by this rule.

The principles of legal interpretation I discuss in this chapter help judges to decide whether these are good arguments about how a particular law should be interpreted.

The results of legal research will reveal many materials requiring legal interpretation. A preliminary evaluation of potential authorities can first be done using the indicators mentioned in the previous chapter. But before presenting any legal materials to a court or tribunal, they must be read carefully to gain a thorough understanding of what they mean in the legal context. Legal interpretation is the skill of bringing out or explaining the meaning of law. It is an essential link between legal research for the purpose of finding potential authorities, and legal communication for the purpose of persuading a decision-maker to accept them as such.

Here is what seems to be a rather simple example of law in the form of a rule:

> Motor vehicles are not allowed in the park.

This prohibition seems straightforward in its meaning, until someone asks whether it applies to the following situations: a motorized lift (cherry-picker) used to trim trees; a police officer on a motorcycle chasing a suspect; or a fire truck called to extinguish a wildfire. In response to such questions, it might be decided that the rule needs to be amended to read:

> Motor vehicles are not allowed in the park, but this does not apply to emergency and maintenance vehicles.

Then a group of veterans asks for permission to install a restored army truck in working condition from the Second World War on a pedestal in the park as a war memorial.[1] Again, there might be a further amendment to the law:

> Motor vehicles are not allowed to be operated in the park, but this does not apply to emergency and maintenance vehicles.

However, more questions continue to be raised, such as: can an elderly person use a motorized chair (scooter) to get around the park? What about a bicycle with a motor assist? What's the status of a motorized wheelchair used by a disabled person? How about a remote-controlled model airplane? Can I use my Segway?[2]

The questions could go on. Should we continue to amend the legislation every time someone thinks of a new possibility? This seems cumbersome and inefficient. A different approach is to allow a judge to decide whether particular situations are covered by the law as they arise and are brought before the court. Taking this approach, laws can be written in general terms, relying on judges and tribunals to decide whether each turn of events is lawful or not when and if it happens. In doing so, judges and tribunals give meaning to the general terms of a law. Legal interpretation thus helps to make written laws workable in practice—it is an effective response to the problem that laws are "incurably incomplete."[3]

In common law systems, legal case analysis—an interpretive operation corresponding to legal interpretation of statutes—is carried out in relation to case decisions, but in a somewhat reverse fashion. Interpretation of legislation starts with general words, and then determines whether they fit or apply to specific situations. However, if there is no relevant legislation, the specific situation under dispute is the starting point from which legal case analysis proceeds in an effort to find precedents. Over the years in a common law system, it may be possible to observe like results in many similar cases; these consistencies in decision-making eventually come to be recognized as *common law rules or principles*. They are that part of the law found in reported decisions and discussed in the textbooks and journal articles. Common law rules and principles are created by drawing out from many particular instances a general statement that summarizes the typical judicial decision; thus the method is the reverse of statutory interpretation, which goes from the general to the particular.

One example of a common law rule is that in order to create a valid contract, all parties must provide *consideration* (something of value) to one another. Over a span of hundreds of years, judges have considered how this rule works in many different situations, and today it is generally accepted as part of the common law in Canada that the consideration given may be minimal in value and need not be proportionate to what is given by the other party. This common law rule for contracts derived from reported cases through legal case analysis may be concisely stated as: in order to form a contract, sufficient consideration (something valuable) must be given, but it need not be adequate (of any particular value). As with most legal rules there is an exception to this one as well. A complementary rule states that a seal affixed to a contract will take the place of consideration required to be given.

Legal case analysis may result in several possible conclusions about the precedent value of a previous case: it is a binding precedent, and must be followed by the judge to reach the same result (the facts of the case are very similar, and it was decided in a higher court); it is an ordinary precedent, and may be followed by the judge if he or she is persuaded to do so (the facts are similar, and it was decided in a court at the same or lower level); it can be distinguished and thus should not be followed (the facts are significantly different, regardless of the level of court that decided it); it may be useful as an analogy (the facts are different, but the result is an appropriate guide for deciding the present case).

Legislative interpretation and common law case analysis introduce flexibility into the law and allow it to adapt to changes in society. Written laws can be interpreted to deal with novel events that legislators couldn't imagine when a law was passed. Similarly, the common law can develop over time without requiring judges to foresee every possible variation of the specific case before them. One English lawyer who later became a famous judge, Lord Mansfield, argued in a case that the common law is able to "work itself pure" by constantly reconsidering and restating its rules and principles as the need arises.[4] However, the methods of statutory interpretation and case analysis also produce uncertainty. In an adversarial system, there is an incentive to promote favourable alternative meanings of legislation and to creatively distinguish unhelpful cases in aid of partisan argument. It is often hard to predict which argument on these issues will prevail. I will discuss the problem of uncertainty in legal outcomes created by legal interpretation later in this chapter and in the next.

The methods of legal interpretation and common law case analysis are taught to law students, but the basic principles of both may be learned by non-lawyers. These ways of working with the law are the foundations of legal argument, and we will examine them in the next chapter.

READING LEGISLATION

Judges read statutes and other forms of legislation in order to apply the law to disputes that come before them. The *application of law* is the process of trying to match facts with legal rules. Sometimes parties will question whether statutory law applies to them, or what the law requires—they argue about its correct interpretation. When judges apply statute law, their judgments may become precedents for future cases decided under the same law. In this way, the meaning of statutes is clarified through legal interpretation. Therefore, precedents are not only useful in relation to common law rules and principles but also to issues of legislative interpretation as well.

Cases that involve the interpretation of legislation are often collected and published together. In Canada, one example of this type of publication is called *Words and Phrases*, which includes judicial interpretations of words found in particular statutes. It is available online through the LawSource commercial database and in law libraries. *Annotated statutes* are published versions of legislation that include *annotations*—citations to cases which have considered particular sections of the statute. The CanLII Canadian open database (and other similar open sources around the world) provides access to precedents for legal interpretation of legislation through links to cases presented alongside the text of the law. Although law dictionaries can be useful in understanding legal terminology, it is best to discover how words in legislation have been interpreted in their specific context by looking for precedents from the courts.

The principles of legal interpretation have evolved over time. At one time, judges followed fixed rules such as the one stating that the literal meaning of legislation, which is grasped solely by looking at the words that have been used, must be accepted and applied even if it leads to an absurd result in the particular case. This *literal meaning rule* and other similar rules of interpretation are sometimes called the *canons of construction*. Many have criticized the rule-based approach to legal interpretation by pointing out that rules are often contradictory and therefore of little assistance in interpretation. To make this point, Karl Llewellyn gave these examples:

Rule	Counter Rule or Exception
Apply the literal meaning	But not if it is contrary to the intent of the statute
Give effect to every word	But not if it is a mistake or inconsistent with the rest of the statute
Follow a grammatical interpretation	But not if it would frustrate the purpose of the law

Recently, Canadian courts have moved away from the rule-based approach to legal interpretation, taking a more flexible one which in Canada has been called the *modern principle (or method) of interpretation*. This method requires judges to pay equal attention to the exact words of the legislative text, their contextual relation to the law as a whole, the intent of the legislators, and the overall purpose of the legislation. In the case *Alberta Union of Provincial Employees v. Lethbridge Community College*[5], the Supreme Court of Canada adopted and approved a method of statutory interpretation described by Elmer Driedger, a law professor at the University of Ottawa, as follows:

> The words of an Act are to be read in their entire context and in their grammatical and ordinary sense harmoniously with the scheme of the Act, the object of the Act, and the intention of Parliament (para. 25)

In this description of the modern method of interpretation, the word *scheme* refers to how the act is organized and designed, *object* refers to the results the act seeks to bring about, and *intention* refers to the social problem the legislators wanted to solve. This approach provides courts with more flexibility when interpreting legislation, including the power to reject the literal meaning of the words used if a different meaning would better carry out the object and intent of the law.

The modern method of interpretation requires specific words to be read in context, which includes the whole of the statute in question and may extend to other legislation as well. Failing to pay attention to the surrounding context of specific words in legislation is one of the mistakes a novice reader of the law can make. It is natural to pay the closest attention to the wording of a particular section of legislation that seems most relevant to the current situation, but the modern method of legal interpretation requires us to expand our reading horizons in order to understand the section in its entire legislative context. Therefore, legislation should be read "from the inside out," starting with the wording of a particular section and working out from there to the rest of the statute, and sometimes to other legislation as well.

A good way to visualize the process of reading statutes is to think of it as the reverse of peeling an onion. Reading should start at the core (the specific words in question) and extend outward to the next larger part of the legislation (the next layer) where the particular section is found, and on to the next layer over that, until reaching the outer "skin" of the legislation as a whole (including the title, and perhaps an introductory section about its purpose). The reader will find the structural components (layers) of a statute, going from the smallest to the largest are: *subclause, clause, subsection, section, division,* and *part.* Figure 8.1 provides an example of the internal structure of one section of an Act.

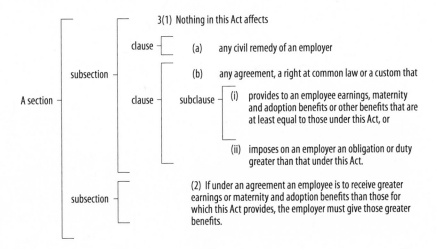

Figure 8.1 Structure of a section of an Act.

This section may be one of many sections within a division of a statute, which along with others may be in a part together with other parts that makes up the whole of the act in question.

Another mistake that those unfamiliar with the law can make when reading legislation is to overlook the existence of *statutory* (or *legislative*) *definitions* contained within it. These are specific sections of legislation that provide definitions of words or phrases found in a statute, regulation, or bylaw. Definitions are often included within legislation to assist with its interpretation; they prescribe the meaning to be used by judges and others when reading it. Statutory definitions have three main purposes: to narrow the meaning of words (e.g., "in this act, 'motor vehicle' means a passenger car"), to expand the meaning (e.g., "in this act, 'motor vehicle' means any vehicle operated by mechanical means capable of transporting a person"), or to give a word a particular and unique meaning (e.g., "in this act, 'motor vehicle' means a commercial vehicle used for the transportation of goods"). Judges must respect such definitions when applying the law, but some interpretation may still be needed—for instance, is a skateboard a vehicle operated by mechanical means?

Statutory definitions may apply throughout a single piece of legislation, or only some parts of it, and some definitions can apply to other statutes. When reading legislation from the inside out, you may encounter definitions that apply only to a certain level of the legislation, such as a section that states "In this part, the word person means. . . ." Many acts have definition sections at the beginning for words or phrases that are used often throughout the legislation. Most jurisdictions also have a separate statute containing definitions for words that are found in many different acts, like "day," "month," and "he." In Alberta, this statute is called the *Interpretation Act*.[6] Here, for example, is the section of that act that explains how definitions in all Alberta legislation are to be read and used when they are included:

Definitions and interpretation provisions

13. Definitions and other interpretation provisions in an enactment [which includes a statute]

(a) are applicable to the whole enactment, including the section containing the definitions or interpretation provisions, except to the extent that a contrary intention appears in the enactment, and

(b) apply to regulations made under the enactment except to the extent that a contrary intention appears in the enactment or in the regulations.

Parliaments and legislatures in many jurisdictions provide online guides and explanations of how legislation is organized and structured, which can be consulted when reading their laws.

Reading a statute "from the inside out," starting with the particular wording you are most concerned with, reveals the context a judge will take into account when considering those words according to the modern method of interpretation. You can also consult a publication like *Words and Phrases,* or an annotated copy of the legislation to discover if there are any precedents concerning the interpretation of the wording in question.

READING CASES

Understanding context is also important when reading a case report. As with legislation, it is easy for a novice reader of legal judgments to get lost in the details of particular cases. Because judges' legal decisions are structured differently than statutes, they should be read "from the outside in" to better appreciate their context. Reading that way leads from the "skin" of a judgment to the "meat and bones" contained within it such as discussion of the parties' arguments, descriptions of the evidence presented by them, and the judge's conclusions regarding these matters. Thus the name of the case reflecting the parties involved in it is found at the beginning, and the ultimate conclusion or order of the court is usually found at the end. The heart of the judgment contains the detailed reasoning followed by the judge to arrive at the ultimate decision. Let's examine the components of a case report in the order in which they should be read.

The name of a reported case is based on the names of the parties involved, and it is a good place to start reading carefully. At the beginning of the case is the *style of cause,* a heading containing the names of the parties involved in the litigation and a description of the roles they have played, such as plaintiff and defendant. If the decision was made by an appeal court, the description *appellant* will be added for the party who appealed the trial decision and *respondent* for the party opposing the appeal. Sometimes both parties appeal different parts of the trial judgment. Note that both a plaintiff and a defendant can usually appeal a decision they do not like. As an example of the structure of a typical reported decision, we will use an important case decided by the Supreme Court of Canada, *Alberta Union of Provincial Employees v. Lethbridge Community College*[7] ("AUPE"). If we look at the report of the AUPE case as decided by the Supreme Court of Canada, we find this style of cause at the beginning:

Board of Governors of Lethbridge Community College, *Appellant*

v.

Alberta Union of Provincial Employees and Sylvia Babin, *Respondents*

and

Canadian Labour Congress, National Union of Public and General Employees and Provincial Health Authorities of Alberta *Interveners*

This tells us that the college appealed, and AUPE opposed the appeal. The *interveners* are parties who are not directly involved in an existing dispute, but who have a strong interest in the outcome of the case, perhaps because it may become a precedent they will have to follow. Interveners therefore may be permitted by the court to present arguments about the issues involved in the action.

The next major section of the report after the style of cause reads as follows:

2003: November 4; 2004: April 29.

Present: McLachlin C.J. and Iacobucci, Major, Bastarache, Binnie, Arbour, LeBel, Deschamps, and Fish J.J.

on appeal from the Court of Appeal for Alberta

This tells us that the case was argued before the court on November 4, 2003 and that the decision was *reserved* (under consideration by the judges) until April 29, 2004, when the judgment was released and published by the court. Finally, we know from this section that the case originated in Alberta, and therefore it will be the law of that particular jurisdiction that will be considered in the judgment.

The next section down states the *catchwords* or *keywords* associated with the decision. These are legal terms describing the general areas of law (for example labor relations) and the main legal concepts (such as jurisdiction) which the judges considered when making the decision. These words often correspond to the subject headings found in legal encyclopedias. Here are the keywords of the AUPE decision:

> Labour relations—Arbitration board—Scope of arbitration board's remedial jurisdiction—Employee dismissed without just cause for non-culpable deficiency—Board awarding damages in lieu of reinstatement—Whether arbitration board could award damages in lieu of reinstatement for dismissal for non-culpable deficiency—Labour Relations Code, R.S.A. 2000, c. L-1, s. 142(2).
>
> Judicial review—Labour relations—Standard of review—Arbitration board—Employee dismissed without just cause for non-culpable deficiency—Board awarding damages in lieu of reinstatement—Standard of review applicable to board's interpretation of remedial provision and to board's award—Labour Relations Code, R.S.A. 2000, c. L-1, s. 142(2).

If the case is a complex one, it may deal with several major areas of law such as "labour relations" and "judicial review" in the AUPE decision.

Next in the case report is the *headnote*, a brief description of the main legal issues presented to the court and the decisions reached on them, with a summary of some of the reasons given by the judges. The headnote may be prepared by the court, or by a publisher in the case of privately printed case reports. Here is a portion of the headnote in the AUPE case:

> The appellant employer had hired the respondent grievor as a scheduling coordinator but dismissed her on the grounds that her work performance was unsatisfactory. The grievor and the respondent union grieved the dismissal, alleging dismissal

without just cause in contravention of the collective agreement. The arbitration board found that, while the grievor was dismissed for non-culpable incompetence, just cause for discharge had not been shown because the employer had failed to comply with the *Re Edith Cavell* criteria setting out the requirements for dismissal of an employee on grounds of non-culpable deficiency. In fashioning the remedy, the majority of the board concluded that it could substitute a financial award under s. 142(2) of the Alberta *Labour Relations Code* and awarded her damages in lieu of reinstatement since reinstatement was inappropriate in the circumstances. The Court of Queen's Bench dismissed the respondents' application for judicial review. The Court of Appeal set that decision aside, ordered that the grievor be reinstated and referred the quantum of back pay to the board for determination. The court found that s. 142(2) did not apply to non-culpable dismissals and that, absent compliance with the *Re Edith Cavell* criteria, the usual and expected remedy was reinstatement.

Held: The appeal should be allowed.

When the relevant factors of the pragmatic and functional approach are properly considered, the standard of review applicable to the arbitration board's interpretation of s. 142(2) of the *Labour Relations Code* and to the board's award is that of reasonableness.

This headnote also gives us some insight into the facts of the case and its history. As stated, this dispute started before an arbitration board, whose decision was appealed first to the Court of Queen's Bench of Alberta and then to the Alberta Court of Appeal, whose decision was in turn appealed to the Supreme Court. We also know from this information that the case involves application of legislation known as the Alberta *Labour Relations Code*, and the legal process of *judicial review* involving the arbitration. However, the conclusion (the *holding*) that "The appeal should be allowed" does not tell us much about what the decision actually means for the parties, other than that the appellant succeeded. The body of the judgment must be read to discover that. Note its beginning words:

The judgment of the Court was delivered by
Iacobucci J.—

This statement indicates that all of the judges who heard this appeal were in agreement because only one judgment was issued by the court, and that one of them, Justice Iacobucci, was designated to write the judgment the other judges *concurred in* (agreed with). If one or more of the judges who heard the case did not agree with the majority, they would prepare a *dissenting judgment*, giving reasons for their view. In a case with a dissent, the decision of the majority would appear first (giving their names) before the dissent. A dissenting judgment can never be used as a precedent. Therefore, it is necessary not to confuse the reasons of the majority of judges with those of the minority. The majority (or unanimous) judgment contains the *ratio decidendi* (or just *ratio*), the reasons for a decision that may be used as precedent in subsequent cases. If the majority comments on a legal issue but does not come to any conclusion about it to reach the final decision, such statements are called *obiter dicta* (or just *obiter* or *dicta*). *Obiter dicta* is not precedent-setting.

What, then, is the actual outcome for the parties in the AUPE case? To find that, look at the end of the judgment where you will find this statement:

VI. Disposition

58. I would allow the appeal with costs throughout, set aside the decision of the Court of Appeal, and restore the award of the majority of the arbitration board.

This statement tells us that after all of the appeals in this case, the original decision of the majority of the arbitrators was judged to be correct. It thus becomes clearer that one of the fundamental issues in this dispute was whether the arbitrators correctly interpreted legislation (the *Labour Relations Code*) in reaching their decision. This information helps to explain why the AUPE case is considered an important precedent regarding legal interpretation in Canada. Before beginning to read the body of the judgment, there is one more part of the "skin" of the text that should be noted. After the headnote there are lists of the cases, legislation, and scholarly writings the court used in reaching its decision. This part of the report provides sources for further research into the issues. Also at the beginning is a brief history of the case, with citations to the decisions of the lower courts that heard it.

The judgment may now be read in detail, but not from beginning to end like a story. The decision of a court is a justification, not a narrative. It attempts to present a comprehensive, persuasive explanation of the result. The reasoning of the court about the core legal issues is the part to pay most attention to when reading a case to determine its value as a precedent. Therefore, a good place to start reading is the section of the judgment that describes the issues:

> IV. Issues
>
> This appeal raises two basic issues. The first concerns the scope of the board's jurisdiction under s. 142(2) of the Code, and the second concerns the exercise of the board's remedial power in light of that jurisdiction. In the reasons that follow, I briefly set out the standard of review against which the board's decision on each issue must be assessed, before turning to analyze the issues themselves.

Since the dispute concerns the correct interpretation of the *Labour Code*, this statement provides further information that the words to be interpreted relate to the jurisdiction of the arbitrators and the powers they are given by the law. If one looks up the term *standard of review* in a legal dictionary, he will discover it means the criteria courts use to decide whether they will overturn the decision of a quasi-judicial decision-making body. From this background, it appears that the Supreme Court had to decide whether the arbitrators' interpretation of the code was faulty. In making that decision, the Supreme Court set a precedent for Canada regarding the correct method of statutory interpretation.

Reading a case report "from the outside in" with a questioning mind yields an appreciation of its impact on the parties involved, the significance it has for the development of the law, and its value as a precedent that may support or detract from a particular legal argument. Once the context of the case is understood—the parties, the legal issues, and the result, it is also possible to read the reasons for the decision from a critical perspective. Do they persuade the reader of the correctness of the result? Are there legal issues that might have been raised, but were not? What impact does the decision have on society generally? These are some of the questions that scholars of critical legal studies may raise when reading cases.

READING CONTRACTS

Judges read contracts to decide whether the parties intended to create mutual legal obligations, and if so, what those require the parties to do. When they are commercial contracts, judges assume agreements are intended to result in some benefit to each party, such as obtaining goods, services, or money. One presumption courts usually follow is that if you sign a document, you agree to everything contained in it, and you know you are assuming legal obligations by doing so.

Therefore when reading contracts:

- Read *before* you sign, seal, open, or click on something, including the proverbial "fine print"
- Read even *what you don't sign* (judges assume you have read what you have been given, such as tickets and receipts)
- Read *everything* (judges assume you have read everything mentioned in a contract, even if it is found in another document or place—this is known as wording *incorporated by reference* in the contract)
- Ask questions *in writing* (oral discussions do not count—this is known as the *parol evidence rule*, which excludes from the contract what is said but not written down); many contracts expressly state they contain all the terms of the agreement, ruling out anything else
- Get answers *in writing* (oral discussions do not count)
- Get everything *in writing* (oral discussions do not count)

Written contracts can suffer from vagueness or ambiguity and "gaps" like legislation. To address these problems, courts have used principles of legal interpretation for contracts in order to identify the intent of the parties at the time of contracting using only the words of the document; to avoid an interpretation that defeats the purpose of the contract even if the words are not ambiguous; to seek an interpretation that makes commercial sense; and to interpret the contract as a whole.

The ideal contract document is the product of a *meeting of minds* with a common intention arrived at through diligent negotiation and careful joint drafting. Very few contracts actually come about that way. Most are *standard forms* written by one party and accepted without scrutiny or objection by another. Some examples of this type of contract are purchase agreements for new vehicles, or leases of houses or apartments. In some jurisdictions, such agreements are called *contracts of adhesion*, meaning that you agree to be bound (adhere) with no possibility of any changes. Standard terms that are used routinely in many contracts of a certain type are called *boilerplate*, meaning traditional wording adopted long ago that is recycled for the sake of convenience and conservatism. Boilerplate is often prevalent in legalese.

Standard form contracts are frequently used in consumer transactions. In some commercial matters, laws have been passed to limit the effect of boilerplate wording, or to incorporate specific wording in contracts to protect the consumer. One example of this intervention by the law is automobile insurance, where definitions and contract terms have been standardized in many jurisdictions for all insurance companies. Another example is airline tickets that include wording and limitations provided in legislation. Critics suggest that boilerplate wording serves commercial interests well because it standardizes transactions, thus making legal rights and responsibilities predictable. From such a perspective, interference by legislators and courts in contract wording and interpretation is inefficient and costly to business.

Judges have always paid close attention to wording in a standard form contract that protects the party who wrote it against claims by the party on the other side of the bargain. This part of an agreement sometimes takes the form of an *exclusion* or *exemption clause*. The usual approach of judges when considering the meaning of such wording is to interpret the protection narrowly. Another principle of contractual interpretation that is sometimes applied by judges in these circumstances is to interpret contracts *contra proferentem*. According to this rule, the party who wrote the contract must bear the consequences of any ambiguity. Judges have also been criticized by business owners for interpreting contracts using this principle.

Special problems of interpretation can arise in contracts that extend over many years, when the circumstances of the parties change considerably from the time of original contracting. In many cases, the parties alter their dealings with each other over time without amending the contract document, or orally agree to amendments that are not put in writing. Long-term agreements are sometimes called *relational contracts* because they generate expectations between the parties based on a sense of relationship that is not merely contractual. Employment contracts of this sort are sometimes interpreted by the courts with more regard for the reasonable expectations of a party than the literal wording of the document. However, some long-term agreements such as treaties with Aboriginal peoples have not been dealt with in this special way.

If the parties clearly express all of their intentions in writing, contracts will be less subject to dispute. However, the courts retain the power to interpret what is written in the public interest. Contracts support the economic life of society, but they may also lead to abuse and unfairness. A critical legal studies perspective can be applied to contract drafting and interpretation to highlight needed reforms.

CRITICAL PERSPECTIVES ON LEGAL INTERPRETATION

Legal interpretation presents a puzzle or paradox for the non-lawyer. When someone becomes involved in a legal dispute, she may expect the law to be clear and straightforward, although she knows that her particular situation is complex and unique. However, when a judge finally hands down the decision that resolves their claim, she finds that the law is described as complex and unclear, and her case is straightforward and routine. What has caused this bewilderment?

Part of the answer lies in the nature of legal decision-making that requires bringing together facts and law. As we saw when discussing framing, the complexities and idiosyncrasies of each case have to be fitted into the conceptual framework of the law. After a judge decides the proper legal categories and characterizations of peoples' actions, he or she may describe the resulting consequences in a judgment as necessary and inevitable. The complexity of life has been refined to yield the clarity of legal facts and lawful results that we call justice. This form of interpretation is more like translation, in which the messy details of concrete reality are repackaged in neat legal concepts, but that is not the focus of this chapter.

The uncertainty of litigation arises from several causes, and a major one is the role played by legal interpretation. The scope of a statute and the strength of a precedent are decided within a judge's wide field of discretion, and the principles of legal interpretation rarely prescribe a single, acceptable result. Critical legal studies scholars may ask why society accepts such a system.

Two types of response have been offered to explain why we accept legal interpretation as part of a legitimate legal order despite the uncertainty that it seems to bring. The first type can be described as apologetic, and the other, critical. An apologetic explanation of legal uncertainty argues that it is to be expected and is therefore normal, given the task of law. A critical explanation attempts to show that uncertainty in interpretation reveals uncomfortable truths about the place of law in society.

The apologetic approach begins by asserting that there is always a generally accepted clear meaning of legal words. The problem is how far words can be "stretched" to fit new situations. This view of interpretation falls within the hermeneutic tradition of scholarship that seeks to discover the true meaning of authoritative texts in order to apply them to current circumstances. One legal philosopher, H.L.A. Hart, explained the task of legal interpretation as sorting out the core meaning of legal terms that are well accepted from their penumbra or surrounding shadow region, where the meaning is uncertain.[8] Ronald Dworkin suggests it is the task of members of the legal community (lawyers, judges, and officials) to make sense of law in areas of uncertainty so as to preserve and extend the integrity (coherence and unity) of law and the legal system.[9] Integrity can make up for uncertainty and thus preserve the legitimacy of the legal system. Another way law may be legitimately uncertain is where unforeseen circumstances arise for which no existing law was expressly intended. These are known as gaps in law, and must be filled through interpretation using analogy and other methods to reach a decision.

Here is an example of interpretation, understood as finding a core meaning that can be affirmed as correct by most members of the legal community and accepted as just by society. The Supreme Court of Canada, in the case *Irwin Toy Ltd. v. Québec (Attorney General)*[10], was required to interpret the word "everyone" found in Section 7 of the Charter of Rights and Freedoms. That section reads,

> 7. Everyone has the right to life, liberty and security of the
> person and the right not to be deprived thereof except in
> accordance with the principles of fundamental justice.

The issue for the court was to decide whether a corporation (Irwin Toy) could claim this right. Although corporations have been recognized in law for a long time, and in many cases have been given the rights and powers of individuals, can "everyone" in this legal context include such artificial persons? The court said "no":

> . . . it appears to us that this section was intended to confer
> protection on a singularly human level. A plain, common sense
> reading of the phrase "Everyone has the right to life, liberty and
> security of the person" serves to underline the human element
> involved; only human beings can enjoy these rights. "Everyone"
> then, must be read in light of the rest of the section and defined
> to exclude corporations and other artificial entities incapable of
> enjoying life, liberty, or security of the person, and include only
> human beings.

The judges are relying on their understanding of what Canadian society considers to be the proper meaning of "everyone" in this particular context. The true meaning is therefore said to be clear ("plain" and "common sense"). Problems can arise with this approach to interpretation, however, in several situations: if there is disagreement on the "plain" meaning within the legal community; if the rest of society does not share the "common sense" of judges or lawyers; or, if society is so diverse that a consensus regarding meaning is elusive.

Two other methods of interpretation that seek the "true meaning" of legislation are known as *originalism* and *textualism*. Originalism in interpretation requires a judge to discover the original intent of the legislators who passed the law, and to follow that despite any subsequent changes in social conditions.

The approach of textualism demands that a judge rely solely on the explicit words of the statute (the "literal meaning") and refuse to consider any matters of policy that might enlarge its scope. Critics have described these hermeneutical styles of interpretation as inherently conservative, and therefore not appropriate in a rapidly changing world.

A critical explanation of the practices of legal interpretation is that, simply put, it is politics by other means—shaped by a judge's interest in securing the result that she considers fair and just. Interpretation is thus guided by the need to provide an acceptable justification for the desired outcome. One problem with this approach is that ideas of justice differ, even among judges. This perspective on legal interpretation has links to the *rhetorical tradition* of scholarship that seeks to justify action by providing persuasive reasons for it. Judging becomes controversial (and sometimes contested) when constitutions or other highly visible statutes (such as criminal laws) are being interpreted. In these cases, judges are sometimes accused of being "activists" and of stepping outside their proper role despite all the good reasons they provide. When disputes involve political questions, the legitimacy of the court as an institution is in danger if judges are suspected of following their own political agendas. Judges can then be criticized for illegitimately making law rather than merely interpreting and applying it. But the question remains of how best to describe the process of legal interpretation—is it the creation or discovery of meaning?

The critical view of interpretation accepts that judges bring their own perspectives, including their attitudes toward public policies, to the task of deciding the meaning of laws. Rather than just expressing a perceived consensus in the community, judges are allowed, and even required to act on their own judgment of what society needs. Judicial decisions should therefore help to persuade the public of the justness of a particular result. The legitimacy of courts can be preserved by effective judicial rhetoric in the form of persuasive reasons for judgment.

One decision of the Supreme Court of Canada provides an example of rhetorical construction of legislation. In what has been colloquially called the Famous Five case[11], the court was asked to decide if the word *person* in sections of the Canadian Constitution concerning the Senate included women within its meaning:

23. The Qualification of a Senator shall be as follows:
   (1) He shall be of the full age of Thirty Years;
   (2) He shall be either a Natural-born Subject of the Queen,
   or a Subject of the Queen naturalized by an Act of the
   Parliament of Great Britain. . . .

24. The Governor General shall from Time to Time, in the
Queen's Name, by Instrument under the Great Seal of Canada,
summon qualified Persons to the Senate; and, subject to the
Provisions of this Act, every Person so summoned shall become
and be a Member of the Senate and a Senator.

The Supreme Court of Canada stated in its decision:

> in considering this matter we are, of course, in no wise [way]
> concerned with the desirability or the undesirability of the
> presence of women in the Senate, nor with any political aspect
> of the question submitted. Our whole duty is to construe, to the
> best of our ability, the relevant provisions of the *BNA Act*, 1867,
> and upon that construction to base our answer. . . .

The court went on to consider another statute that stated the word "he" in
legislation should be interpreted to also mean "she." Here, the court quoted
from and agreed with an earlier judgment:

> It is sufficient to say that the Legislature, in dealing with this
> matter, cannot be taken to have departed from the usage of
> centuries or to have employed such loose and ambiguous words
> to carry out so momentous a revolution in the constitution of
> this House.

In other words, the centuries'-old policy of excluding women from political life should not be disturbed by "loose and ambiguous" words such as "he
includes she." Such a revolution was beyond the imagination of these judges.

However, this decision was appealed to the House of Lords in Britain, which at the time could still overrule the Supreme Court of Canada. In *Edwards v. A.G. of Canada*[12], the Law Lords (judges of the House of Lords) reversed the judgment, and allowed women to become senators, stating:

> The word "person" as above mentioned may include members of both sexes, and to those who ask why the word should include females, the obvious answer is why should it not.
> [and having regard to]
>
> 1. To the object of the Act, viz., to provide a constitution for Canada, a responsible
>   and developing state;
>
> 2. that the word "person" is ambiguous and may include members of either sex. . . .
>   women are eligible to be summoned to and become members of the Senate of Canada.

The policy perspectives of the English judges and their desire to see a result that the Supreme Court of Canada did not criticize, but would not sanction, led to a watershed decision in Canadian law. Indeed, this British decision described the Canadian Constitution as a "living tree," capable of growth and development—a view that clearly departs from originalist and textualist approaches to interpretation. The critical view of interpretation poses a further question, however, whether we are happy to accept results we do not agree with as well as those we do.

Some have criticized the policy-oriented style of interpretation as being *judicial law-making, judicial activism,* or *judicial interference* with the wishes of the democratic majority as expressed in legislation. It is considered a liberal approach to interpretation in contrast to the conservative approaches of originalism and textualism. The modern method of interpretation in Canada seems to have combined aspects of several of these and other approaches, but it is clear that Canada's judges pay close attention to the policy and purpose of legislation.

Understanding and skill in using the techniques of legal interpretation equips both students of legal studies and litigants to better understand judges' reasoning and to present critical and persuasive arguments.

After reading this chapter you should be able to:

- explain what is meant by a conservative and a liberal approach to legal interpretation by judges
- describe a method for reading legislation and explain the legal context in which specific legislation operates
- explain what is meant by the modern method of interpretation
- describe a method for reading cases and explain the legal context in which a specific case may be considered a precedent
- explain the concepts of reasons for decision, *obiter dicta*, and dissent
- describe a method for reading contracts and explain the legal rights and obligations in a specific contract
- explain the parol evidence rule and the principle of *contra proferentem* in relation to contract interpretation

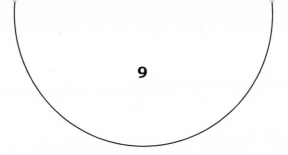

9

LEGAL COMMUNICATION

Oral and Written Communication
to Achieve Legal Objectives

Legal communication builds on all of the other tools of legal literacy discussed in this book. Effective communication in a legal context allows students of legal studies and litigants to describe (frame) people's needs and concerns using the concepts and terminology of the law; locate the legal institution (court or administrative body) with jurisdiction to respond to them; identify and plan the steps to be taken in legal processes (court or administrative procedures); prepare for those steps and take them (using documents and communications) when required; find, present, and explain the legal materials (legislation and cases) that operate as authorities; make well-organized and persuasive arguments (about facts and law) to decision-makers, and advocate coherent ideas and proposals for improving law and the legal system.

Legal communication also occurs both in adversarial and *transactional* contexts, required to achieve the legal goals of making a will, negotiating a contract, or offering to buy property. However, if challenged, these and other transactions will require legal proceedings either to implement or undo them. This chapter focuses on communication for the purpose of assisting judges and tribunals to resolve legal disputes of all kinds, whether arising from contracts, accidents, or other causes.

PROOF OF FACTS IN LAW

Legal decision-makers refuse to decide hypothetical questions. The judicial (and quasi-judicial) role is to apply the law to real situations that have given rise to specific disputes. Legal decisions are therefore based on the facts of particular circumstances, actions, or events. In litigation therefore, judges must first gain knowledge of these factual matters, then proceed to consider which law should be applied and what it requires. Thus communication between disputing parties and decision-makers is required to reveal the facts of the matter; discover the relevant law; decide how the law applies to the facts; and determine the consequences of that application.

The resulting judgment or order will state the decisions that have been made on all of these matters, including findings of fact. It is therefore inaccurate to talk about communicating facts to courts or tribunals. Legally speaking, there are no facts in a case until a decision about them has been made. Another way of putting this is to say that only proven facts are considered for the purpose of deciding the current case.

Evidence is the information communicated by the parties to the decision-maker in order to prove facts. Here's an example: when applying for a passport, it is necessary to prove a place of birth in order to establish citizenship. An oral statement based on family history and tradition will not be enough for the passport office—this evidence is not sufficient proof of the fact of citizenship. Instead, documentary evidence such as birth certificate will probably be required to support a finding of citizenship and therefore of entitlement to a passport.

Before the facts are found (concluded to be proved) by a decision-maker, they are only allegations, or suggestions of what the facts are. When information is presented by the parties, it must first be admitted as evidence by the decision-maker, which means it will be taken into consideration when deciding the facts. The admissibility of certain evidence may be opposed by the other side in an adversarial matter, when they do not wish it to be used. Witnesses who can prove they are experts are allowed to give opinions on technical matters, but ordinary witnesses must stick to reporting only what they have experienced through any of their senses (sight, hearing, etc.). If evidence is decided to be inadmissible, then it will not be considered further when finding the facts. When considering which alleged facts have been proved, a decision-maker may accept some or all of the admitted evidence. Evidence that is accepted is taken to be truthful and valuable. A judge or tribunal then weighs all of the accepted evidence to evaluate its contribution in convincing the decision-maker(s) which facts have been sufficiently proved. Note that information is not evidence until it is admitted, admitted evidence may not ultimately be accepted, and only evidence that has been admitted and accepted will be weighed (evaluated) when determining the facts.

The facts stated in the decision of a legal dispute are not necessarily the same as the truth of what happened. They are only that portion of the truth which can be proved by evidence. And there is yet another restriction on the facts in legal proceedings: only some facts are relevant, or legally worth considering, when making a decision. The relevancy of a fact is determined by the legal issue to be decided and the applicable law. If a fact is not related by logic or in any other way to the legal question, then it will be disregarded in making that decision. For example, the fact that an applicant is a doctor is not relevant when making the decision whether he or she should be given a passport.

The world of legally proven facts is therefore a virtual one, and the people in it are like avatars—they do not have all the depth and detail of living persons. This is why people may not recognize themselves or the truth of their circumstances in the facts recited in a legal judgment. The law adopts a model of how people are expected to act, and the legal system ensures conformity to it. In the "game-world" of law, a pre-programmed fact scenario recognized as familiar by the legal system may determine the legal outcome even though the truth may be more complex.

Law schools teach budding lawyers to be objective, dispassionate, and professional. These traits may lead lawyers to ignore the social context and personal meaning of events to their clients, and focus solely on the legally relevant (and provable) facts. What is not legally relevant is inconsequential. As a result, lawyers begin to view people solely in terms of their legal roles and legally recognized relationships, and judges may follow suit. The technical requirements of the legal system thus take priority over the needs and concerns of the public. In this process, perspectives are reframed in legal terms such that the original voices of clients are muted and their real "story" is lost in the legal facts.

Litigants without lawyers usually have no hesitation in telling their full stories to legal decision-makers. Courts and tribunals may allow more latitude to such parties when presenting their evidence. Nevertheless, a self-represented party may be stopped at some point if he or she clearly fails to follow the rules for proving facts that form part of the law of evidence. The best known restriction on the admissibility of evidence in this area of law is the rule against admitting hearsay as evidence, which is repeating information stated by someone who is not present (e.g., "John told me he saw the light was yellow when I went through the intersection"). Hearsay is second- or third-hand information. The hearsay rule demonstrates the legal preference for evidence given in person by witnesses who directly observed or participated in the events in question. In many administrative tribunals and agencies, the strict rules of evidence (such as the hearsay rule) are not enforced, and facts may be proved through hearsay and other less formal means such as affidavits (sworn statements in writing).

The results of most legal disputes are determined by the facts found by the decision-maker: a party has either proved all the necessary relevant facts, or has not. Whether the rules of evidence are enforced or not, it is still up to the person who has the burden (responsibility or onus) of proof to offer admissible, believable, and sufficient evidence of all facts he or she must prove. In most cases, the person who alleges a fact must prove it. The burden of proof is the duty to prove everything you allege as a fact. The standard of proof is the degree of certainty the court or tribunal requires before finding a fact to be proved. In civil proceedings, the standard of proof is described as a balance of probabilities: based on all the relevant evidence, it is more likely than not that a particular fact is the truth of the matter. In criminal matters, a higher standard, proof beyond a reasonable doubt (leaving no real doubt in one's mind) is required.

In summary, legal communications about disputed facts involve a burden to provide sufficient information that will be admitted as evidence and accepted as truthful in order to prove all the relevant facts according to the standard of proof required in the legal proceedings.

LEGAL ARGUMENT

Legal argument consists of ideas presented as the best way to arrive at a rational answer to a question faced by a legal decision-maker. The questions that need to be answered depend on the legal issue involved. Issues in disputed cases usually involve questions of fact, and sometimes questions of law. Legal questions take various forms, such as:

What facts have been proved, and by whom?
What is the appropriate law to apply to this case?
How is the law to be interpreted and applied?
What should be done according to the law as applied to this case?

There are different forms of argument for each type of question that arises in legal decision-making.

First, let's consider questions of fact. Arguments about facts are based on the *inferences* (conclusions that fill gaps) that should be drawn from the evidence admitted by the decision-maker. In some situations, there may be an independent eyewitness who observed all of the events in question. If there are no doubts about that person's memory, eyesight, honesty, or impartiality that may affect his or her *credibility* (believability), then there is little to argue about concerning the information provided in the testimony. What such a witness reports will usually be accepted by the decision-maker as good proof of the facts they speak about.

In cases where there is no such convincing proof, then a *factual argument* may be presented. Argument about facts is based on reasoning about probability. Given the statements of witnesses, available documents, and all other admitted evidence, what is the most probable reconstruction of what actually happened? In considering this question of probability, a decision-maker will rely on his or her common sense, understanding of human nature, experience of similar events, and knowledge of procedures and processes that are usually followed in similar situations. Arguments about facts should therefore appeal to these ways of thinking. Factual arguments may take these forms:

It makes good sense to conclude that things happened this way.
Human nature tells us that people usually act in this way in such circumstances.
We know that people usually follow this approach when in this situation.

An argument of fact invites the decision-maker to infer that things probably happened the way the speaker or writer suggests, and that such a conclusion makes sense, taking into account all of the evidence.

Next, let's look at argument concerning questions of law. Law takes different forms, and each calls for a unique method of argument. Rules are perhaps the most common form of law, and certain types of argument are useful when they are disputed. A threshold issue in any legal dispute is jurisdiction—the question of whether the decision-making body has the authority to deal with the case and to give the requested *remedy* (or *relief*). Jurisdiction is frequently defined by rules. For example, "A claim for damages under $10,000 shall be made in the small claims court"; or, "An appeal must be filed in writing with the Board within 14 days of receiving notice of a decision."

These rules prescribe which legal institution has jurisdiction over a certain type of claim, and what must be done before a decision-making body has jurisdiction to hear an appeal. Rules often use the words *must* or *shall*, which usually mean something is *mandatory* (required and not optional).

The most frequent questions to be answered by decision-makers about rules (jurisdictional or otherwise) are: "Which rule governs the situation?" and "How should the rule be interpreted?" The first question is often determined by the way the legal issue is framed. Let's take as an example unusually damaging contact between players in a professional sports game. The situation may be framed (characterized) as a *tort* (non-criminal infliction of harm), or as a criminal offence, or both. If the event is framed as a tort, then the civil law of assault and battery would apply, and if as a crime, then criminal law would be applicable.

As I discussed in the previous chapter, Canadian courts look to the purpose of legislation as a guide when questions arise about its proper interpretation. *Interpretive arguments* therefore may suggest that statutory wording should be given a certain meaning, because the result of doing so would carry out the intention of the lawmakers and fulfill the purpose of the legislation. In addition to the surrounding context, arguments about legal interpretation should also deal with the precise wording of the law in question to respond to concerns of a decision-maker who takes a textual approach to interpretation. The question as to how a legal rule applies to a specific fact often calls for argument based on legal *deductive reasoning* in the form of a *syllogism*, which will be discussed in the final section of this chapter.

In addition to rules, law can also take the form of *discretion, standards* (sometimes called tests), and *principles*; there are types of argument appropriate for each. Discretion may be divided into two types: *unfettered discretion* (unconstrained authority to decide), and *discretion according to law*. Someone who has unfettered discretion (such as a government minister in some situations) may make a decision based upon whatever factors he or she considers relevant and important. If one is allowed to make arguments to such a decision-maker, they are not legal arguments in the same sense as those made to a judge, and the courts will not interfere in such decisions. Conversely, some decision-makers (such as administrative boards and tribunals) are given discretion to decide within legal limits. These limits are set by *policy*, situational factors, or any relevant considerations. Discretionary decisions made according to law must respect such limits, and the courts will intervene if the legal guidelines for decision-making are ignored or overstepped. *Predictive reasoning* may be used to foresee the effect of making a decision one way or the other. Arguments about how to exercise discretion according to law may therefore highlight the probable effects of deciding in a particular way:

> It would promote (or frustrate) important policy to decide in this way because of the likely consequences, such as. . . .

> The legislation requires you to take the following matters into account in making your decision, and they support our position in this matter.

> Here are some relevant factors you should consider in exercising your discretion, which you will see point to a decision in our favour.

One clue that discretion is involved in decision-making is the use of words such as *may, in its opinion, in its view,* or *decide having regard to the following matters*. Terminology like this means that a decision-maker has the authority to make a particular decision, but is not required to do so.

Tests or standards are a form of law often found in the common law as it has developed over centuries. These are common law rules or principles that judges have found necessary in areas of law such as torts and contracts to establish legal rights and obligations. Sometimes the requirements of tests or standards are described as the *elements* that must be shown to exist to make a claim. For example, to be successful in a claim involving the tort of *negligence,* it must be shown that the defendant had a duty to take care, that there was a breach of that duty, and that damage (harm) resulted. Duty, breach, and damage are considered the basic elements of the tort of negligence, although the law is more complex than this. Because common law tests or standards are drawn from precedents, one appropriate way of arguing about them is to use *analogical reasoning* (reasoning based on similarity). Arguments by analogy are intended to show that the question to be answered has been decided before by a precedent, or even if the facts are quite different, that the previous case nevertheless provides good guidance although not a precedent. The counter-argument regarding analogy is to distinguish a previous case—to show how it is significantly different from the present one, and therefore shouldn't be considered a precedent or even useful as a guide. Arguments about common law legal tests or standards may be phrased in the following ways:

The test to be applied in this case is met in the following ways. . . .

All of the elements required to answer this question in our favour are found here as follows. . . .

The facts in this case are substantially the same as (different from) those in the case of . . . which should (not) be considered as a precedent; therefore the decision here should (not) be the same.

If legislation is not relevant and cases are used as statements of the law, then the legal issue probably concerns a common law test or standard. However, standards are also sometimes found in laws such as *building standards* and *safety codes*. These types of standard are actually rules created by legislation.

Lastly, law may take the form of general *legal principles*. Because principles are general statements, there are often no situational factors, guidelines, tests, or elements added to them to guide decision-makers. Sometimes different legal principles seem to lead to opposite decisions in a particular case. The scope of application of principles is also sometimes in doubt. One form of argument that is appropriate when dealing with legal principles concerns consistency or compatibility—whether a particular foreseeable result would or would not be in harmony with a principle. *Balancing* is another form of argument that responds to the problem of competing principles. A legal principle can usually be paired up against one or more opposing ones (like the rules of legal inter-pretation), leading to an argument that one is more important in the particular circumstances. Arguments about legal principles can therefore be constructed in these terms:

> The principle should (not) be extended to cover a situation like this.

> It would be (in)consistent with the principle to decide this way for the following reasons. . . .

> When balancing the principles in this situation, the principle of . . . should be given more importance because. . . .

Sometimes legal principles are expressed in the form of rights, such as those found in the Canadian Charter of Rights and Freedoms, and in consti-tutional documents in other countries. However, not all principles are found in legislation. The *principles of natural justice,* for instance, were developed by courts through precedent to ensure fair administrative decision-making according to law.

A single legal issue in a relatively simple situation will usually require some factual argument, plus one or two arguments about the law. A complex dispute with many legal issues and extensive, conflicting evidence may call for all the types of argument I have defined. For every argument made, the other side will likely have a counter-argument.

LEGAL WRITING

Lawyers write many things: legislation, contracts, wills, pleadings filed with courts, letters to their clients, and demands for the payment of debts. All of these documents can be considered as legal writing. The focus in this section, however, will be on writing that contains legal arguments. Such documents are usually called *written submissions* (or *written argument*) in Canada, and *briefs* in the United States.

Law is expected to be rational, based on comprehensible ideas and logical thought. Legal arguments accordingly use legal concepts, and deductive, inductive, analogical, and other types of reasoning to provide answers to legal questions. Emotions such as feelings of sympathy or disgust are not legitimate grounds for answering legal questions because they are considered irrational. The rule of law requires legal decisions to be made according to legal rules and principles, not personal feelings or preferences. But it is not correct to say that emotions must be disregarded in legal writing. Written submissions may contain more than just rational arguments.

Justice Scalia of the United States Supreme Court and his co-author suggest that legal argument should invoke moral approval, perceptions of justice, and reasonableness in addition to providing technical legal answers for the issues to be decided.[1] These experts and others agree that good legal writing may appeal to the emotions of a decision-maker as well as to their intellect. Thus, argumentative legal writing is rhetorical—it is intended to motivate the reader (a judge or tribunal) to take a desired course of action. Chief Justice McLachlin of the Supreme Court of Canada describes it simply as "communication that convinces."[2] If persuasive legal writing were solely based on logic and rational thought, it might be possible to construct a computer program to evaluate the arguments presented and reach a decision. Many, however, would probably be uncomfortable allowing a computer to dispense justice. For instance, a legal artificial intelligence software program might logically decide to evict a widow and her children from their apartment on Christmas Eve, but it is difficult to imagine a human(e) judge doing so.[3] We value decision-makers who are not only rational but also sensitive to emotions and perceptions of justice. It would not make sense to try to stimulate positive feelings in a computer, but it is worthwhile when writing for judges and other legal decision-makers.

Let's consider some recommendations that have been made for making legal writing persuasive. They can be grouped into three broad topics of concern: those focusing on the audience for legal writing and its context; recommendations directed to the structure and organization of such writing; and lastly, suggestions concerning the contents and mode of expression.

Judges are the most important audience for persuasive legal writing, and they have often been stereotyped as conservative "nit-pickers"—concerned with details, precision, and formalities. Non-lawyers writing legal arguments will probably not be held to the same standards as legal professionals, but they should still keep the character of this audience in mind. Judges need to understand the argument being made, which encourages their use of the proper method to make a decision, and they must also feel that the desired result will be just, which gives them the motivation to decide as requested. As with all writing, good grammar, correct spelling, and proper citation of legal authorities enhances the credibility of the writer and thus contributes to the persuasiveness of the submission. The context of legal writing is potentially the whole of the legal system, together with all the relevant concepts, rules, and principles. Non-lawyers are at a disadvantage when trying to integrate argument into relevant legal contexts, but basic knowledge of the key laws and principles may be enough to get by. Writers with limited legal knowledge are well advised not to use unfamiliar words or legalese that may have unforeseen (and unfortunate) meanings and legal consequences in the context where they are presented.

There is one simple but important recommendation for structuring a written submission: make sure it has one. This means organizing arguments and other material in sections using headings, points, and other methods to provide a clear and coherent framework for the document. Many courts regulate the form and contents of written submissions. In the Supreme Court of Canada, such documents are called *factums*, and according to the court's rules they should be structured in the following order: Title; Table of Contents; Overview of Facts; Issues; Argument; Costs; Orders Sought; Table of Authorities; and, lastly, Statutes, Rule.

Today, factums filed with the Supreme Court of Canada and many other courts are available on the courts' websites, providing examples of good persuasive legal writing.

Informal decision-makers, such as administrative boards and tribunals, often do not have such strict rules about the form and structure of written argument. In these forums, it will usually be acceptable if a submission includes four sections corresponding to the basic parts of any legal argument:

1. A statement of the legal issue or issues that must be decided (using the technique of framing)

2. Discussion of the facts to be proved and the evidence presented to accomplish that goal (factual argument)

3. Argument concerning the law to be applied (selection, interpretation, and application of the relevant law)

4. Conclusion and request (the desired decision or action to be taken)

Each section of a legal argument should contain cross-references to the others, showing how the law applies to the facts and leads to the requested result. A written submission in a complex case may deal separately with several legal issues, using the four sections listed for each one. Sometimes one issue will depend on the answer to another so that submissions may contain "nested" sub-arguments, such as "if this argument is accepted, it leads on to a further issue which must then be decided."

Good written submissions should include counter-arguments to points one side anticipates the other side will make, which can be integrated with the main arguments presented in a separate section. Most legal writing experts recommend presenting the strongest arguments first and the conclusion to be drawn from them, followed by an explanation of why they should be accepted. Overall, the basic points or general context should come before specifics and details. Legal argument should not simply regurgitate the research an individual has conducted, but rather present an orderly arrangement of ideas leading to the desired conclusion. There is no single correct structure for a written submission, but if it contains well-organized sections dealing with the issues, facts, law, and requests, it will likely be a persuasive document that is taken seriously by any legal decision-maker.

A written submission may appeal to a decision-maker's emotions and perceptions of justice. This type of persuasive writing can be integrated in a legal submission when discussing the facts.[4] Consider two different openings describing the facts of the same case: "The plaintiff is a pensioner residing in subsidized housing," or "The plaintiff is Esther Peabody. She is 81 years of age and a widow. Her health is not good and she can only afford to live in this studio apartment because her rent is subsidized by the government." The second description starts to paint a picture that evokes sympathy, while the first is a cold and abstract statement framing the situation using only bare legal concepts. If the case concerns a dispute with the landlord, the second, more humanized version gives the decision-maker some motivation to find a justifiable way to decide in the tenant's favour.

Legal writing teachers recommend that the discussion of the facts in a written submission should take the form of a narrative rather than simply a list of details. A narrative encourages the reader to see the party about whom it is written as an individual with a unique history and perspective on the events in question. Two strategies writers can use when developing a narrative that may appeal to a legal reader are: to draw an analogy to a classic storyline that evokes sympathy (such as Scrooge and Tiny Tim), or to describe the party as a typical underdog who deserves to be heard and treated fairly (like David and Goliath). Such a strategy when presenting the facts is sometimes called the theme or theory of the submission. Mrs. Peabody's case, for instance, might be likened to a contest between David (an isolated individual) and Goliath (a powerful corporation). If Mrs. Peabody was disabled and could not find other accessible accommodation, then she might be considered a member of a minority group whose voice was not sufficiently heard. A legal narrative, however, must not be fiction—it must include all of the relevant facts, and not simply ignore inconvenient ones. One sure way to lose the sympathy of a judge is to lose track of the truth.

Persuasive legal writing is one important nexus of law and society—good written arguments can challenge decision-makers to find ways to mould the law to meet society's needs. Judges are human, and should always be reminded that the parties who appear before them are human too.

LEGAL SPEECH

The principles of natural justice require that the parties involved in legal proceedings be given an opportunity to state their case and answer any opposing arguments. Sometimes that is done by way of written submissions, sometimes by oral presentations, and in some cases a combination of the two. This section focusses on *oral argument* (or *oral submissions*) made to a legal decision-maker.

In a debate between politicians in a Parliament or other legislative body, speeches are addressed to the presiding officer, often called the Speaker. Similarly, in legal matters communications should be directed to the judge or other presiding official, not to other parties. This practice is intended to allow everyone to make their oral submissions in an orderly manner. If there are opposing parties, the party who started the proceedings will usually go first, followed by the other side, with an opportunity at the end for the first party to respond to what they have heard (sometimes called *reply* or *rebuttal*).

The degree of a hearing's formality in a legal matter varies among decision-making bodies (courts being the most formal), but experts recommend that an oral argument should be more like engaging in a discussion rather than making a speech.[5] This advice is a reminder that the judge or tribunal expects assistance from the parties to make a good decision. For that reason, a judge or member of a tribunal may respond to oral submissions by asking questions or commenting on the points that are made. Such interactions are a good indication as to whether the decision-maker understands the arguments, and where they see problems in the presentation. This discussion with a decision-maker permits clarification and further efforts at persuasion.

A person representing themselves without a lawyer can use oral argument to tell his story in a way that motivates the decision-maker to decide in his favour. He can explain the history and background of the case from a perspective which shows that the requested decision makes good sense and is fair and reasonable. Of course, he must also include legal arguments which will convince the decision-maker that the desired result is legally justifiable. If done effectively, statements made in oral argument will sometimes be repeated by a judge as part of the decision.

Here are some practical recommendations from legal experts on how to act when making an oral presentation: be sure use the correct *form of address* (respectful description) for the judge or other official to whom you are making your presentation (e.g., "Your Honour," "My Lord," "Madam Chair"); if in doubt, ask for guidance[6]; be aware of body language—what posture and movements indicate about yourself and the decision-maker (do not fidget); maintain eye contact with all of the decision-makers to establish your credibility and gain empathy for your arguments.[7]

Robert Barr Smith recommends that someone giving an oral argument should behave in a civilized way by speaking respectfully about all present, including any opposed parties

- be direct and be yourself; don't pretend to be a lawyer or try to act like you think one would
- write out your argument, or have your written submission in front of you, but don't read it; use your notes as a prompt while maintaining eye contact
- never interrupt another speaker (especially the decision-maker!); if you are interrupted, stop immediately and wait for direction to continue.[8]

Finally, Antonin Scalia and Bryan A. Garner give this advice:

- organize and index all the written materials you will refer to; make copies for everybody, including any other parties
- be sure any visual aids are working and that you know how to use them

- dress appropriately
- be conversational but not familiar
- make your strongest argument first
- welcome questions, listen to them carefully, and answer immediately; don't put them off until later
- if you don't know the answer to a question, say so; don't guess or say something you're not sure of
- recognize friendly questions intended to help you better present your case
- never question the decision-maker except about procedure
- be prepared to discuss hypothetical situations and how they relate to your case if they are mentioned by the decision-maker
- be prepared to change the order of your argument if the decision-maker's questions require it
- never become impatient or hostile if the decision-maker disagrees with you; make your best argument and move on
- don't agree with a suggestion from the decision-maker unless you are sure it could not hurt your argument; don't concede just to be amiable
- when you have nothing useful left to say, stop talking
- say "thank you for listening" when you finish.[9]

Arguments may be adjusted and rephrased when making oral submissions in response to the needs and concerns expressed by the decision-maker in a way that is not possible in writing. A case may be won or lost because of an oral presenter's ability, or lack of it, to answer questions and consider hypothetical situations. The core value of oral argument is that it allows the humanity of the parties to shine through. The best preparation for making an oral submission is to observe others presenting their cases to the decision-maker. If the hearings are not open to the public, the court or tribunal staff will usually describe what happens in an oral setting. Some decision-making bodies have placed videos of a typical hearing on their websites to provide guidance for parties appearing before them.

A good oral argument may help to change the law for the benefit of the party making it and for others who may have similar legal problems.

Good communicators take their audience seriously—they keep in mind the needs, assumptions, knowledge, and ways of thinking of their readers and listeners. Accordingly, legal communication should demonstrate understanding of the primary legal audience: judges, lawyers, tribunal members, and administrative officials. Previous chapters have provided an introduction to some of the important concepts, ideas, language, systems, and structures of the law. This section describes some of the ways members of the legal community typically think and communicate, insights that should be taken into account when presenting legal arguments to them.

Lawyers are expert communicators within the legal system. Can non-lawyers be as effective in communicating their own legal needs and interests? Is there something unique, mysterious, and difficult about the way lawyers think that gives them an advantage? Critics have given conflicting answers to these questions which we will explore below.

Law schools have traditionally described their mission as teaching law students "to think like lawyers." Is "thinking like a lawyer" different from thinking like any other rational person? To help answer this question, we can examine three common thought processes found in law and other disciplines: *deductive, inductive,* and *analogical reasoning.*

Deductive reasoning (moving logically from one truth to another) is familiar in mathematics and takes the form of a *syllogism* (logical train of thought) demonstrated in this classic example:

> Major premise: All humans are mortal.
> Minor premise: All Greeks are humans.
> Conclusion: All Greeks are mortal.

Deductive reasoning thus involves going from generalizations to more specific instances that logically flow from the starting point. In law, it may be used when applying rules like this:

> Major premise: Failing to stop at a red light is an offence.
> Minor premise: You drove your car through a red light.
> Conclusion: You are guilty of an offence.

This example seems to show that deductive reasoning is no different in law than in other areas. Some critics, however, point out that it is more correct to word a legal syllogism as follows:

> Failing to stop at a red light is an offence, but in some cases drivers may have a lawful excuse or exemption from the law.
>
> If proved: that the light was red; that it was you who was driving; and you have no legal excuse or exemption.
>
> Then you are guilty of an offence.

Describing the chain of reasoning in this way brings out the difference between statements that are simply assumed to be true, and propositions of law and fact that can be disputed. For instance, what if the vehicle in question was an unmarked police car responding to a 911 call? What might be the legal result if the vehicle had been hijacked by a passenger pointing a gun at the driver? The steps in legal deductive reasoning are always only provisional and subject to proof and exceptions. A legal syllogism therefore lacks some of the logical necessity associated with mathematics, but this form of reasoning is nevertheless well accepted in law. This leaves open the question, however, of whether legal deductive reasoning is a unique way of thinking.

Inductive reasoning (arriving at generalities based on specifics) is common in science. One famous story tells how Isaac Newton observed apples and other objects drop to the ground, and concluded there must be a general principle at work, thus "discovering" gravity. In law, inductive reasoning is primarily found in the development of rules and principles of the common law. A judge who considers past decisions made over many years may conclude they demonstrate a general principle that can be used to decide the current case. Inductive reasoning of this type can add something new to the common law. This is exactly what happened in the (legally) famous case of *Donoghue v. Stevenson*.[10] In that decision, the British House of Lords reviewed many past decisions about harm inflicted on one person by another, and concluded that the *neighbour principle* is the basis of all claims for compensation arising out of the tort of negligence. According to this principle, a person's neighbour, legally speaking, is anyone that person should have in mind who may potentially be harmed by his or her actions. This landmark case resulted in a more generalized statement of the common law of negligence based upon an inductive mode of thought.

Some observers find induction in law to be almost mystical, and have described it as the reflection of changing social views in the minds of individual judges.[11] Others find it less mysterious. Law schools have paid special attention to inductive reasoning, which they call *case synthesis* (forming a general idea based on a variety of decisions), so it has become one of the hallmarks of thinking like a lawyer. Knowing many past cases and having the ability to compare their facts in a detailed and organized way is important for legal inductive thinking. Perhaps there is also an element of insight or intuition in arriving at a new legal idea like the neighbour principle. It remains an open question whether the inductive method in legal reasoning makes legal thought unique.

Finally, legal *analogical reasoning* (drawing useful comparisons) is sometimes described as the most unique aspect of thinking like a lawyer. Analogies are used in legal thinking to fill gaps in the law where it is uncertain which legal rule or principle should be used, or when a law is vague or ambiguous. Finding a good analogy is similar to comparing the details of past decisions in inductive reasoning, but the goal is different. Making an analogy allows a rule used in one case to be borrowed for use in a different (but comparable) one. Analogies do not usually result in new rules or principles, but they extend the range of application of existing law to new situations.

Creative analogical reasoning in law can be described as an art similar to a poet's choice of evocative metaphors and similes. Scott Brewer, however, describes the legal method of using analogies (*exemplary reasoning* is his term for it) as merely another form of rational thinking that attempts to identify important similarities (for legal purposes) in different fact situations.[12] Perhaps it is right to call legal analogizing an art form. It does require knowledge of rules and cases in areas of law that are ripe to be borrowed, and imagination to make the connection.

Frederick F. Schauer's view is that the idea of making a decision consistent with established law, although it may seem somewhat unfair or unjust in the specific situation at hand, is one unique aspect of legal thought. He describes this as putting systemic values (such as following precedent) above concern for making the best decision in the immediate circumstances.[13] Michael Scriven, however, points out that all disciplines have rules to safeguard system values (such as statistical thresholds of significance) that arguably frustrate systemic goals like the search for truth or justice.[14] Competing values and goals that influence thought processes can be found in all professional realms, not just law.

Perhaps it is the combination of all of these methods of thought, supplemented by insights and intuitions, which make legal reasoning appear special. Or is it just another example of the complex problem-solving found in most professions? James F. Stratman points to the dynamic complexity of the social and argumentative field in which lawyers work—having to anticipate the counter-arguments of opposing lawyers, as well as the synthesizing influence of the court.[15] From a critical legal studies perspective, we should be wary of professional claims to esoteric knowledge and unique skills that serve to elevate and insulate lawyers and judges from the rest of society.

As in other complex human endeavours, perhaps the greatest mystery is how legal problems are formulated in the first place. That returns us to the practice of framing life in legal terms and the necessary interplay of law and society with which this book started.

CHAPTER REVIEW

After reading this chapter you should be able to:

- describe the role of deductive, inductive, and analogical reasoning in legal thought
- explain the difference between factual and legal issues
- explain the concepts of facts, evidence, burden of proof and standard of proof
- describe the principal types of legal issues and the methods of argument appropriate to them
- describe the basic structure of a written argument or submission
- list some guidelines for making an oral legal argument
- prepare a basic written submission to assist legal decision making including the following parts: issues raised, relevant law, evidence presented, argument of law and fact, and decision requested

NOTES

CHAPTER 1: INTRODUCTION

1   A loose group of American law professors have been labelled the Critical Legal
     Studies Movement ("Crits" for short). The term "critical legal studies" as used
     in this book is not intended to refer to them, although the critical approach
     presented here has something in common with their work. Like the Crits, this
     text raises questions about the proper relation of law to society, but unlike
     them, it does not propose wide ranging changes to law and the legal system
     pursuant to a vision inspired by leftist politics.

2   *Constitution Act 1982* [en. by the *Canada Act 1982* (UK), c. 11, s. 1] pt. I (*Canadian
     Charter of Rights and Freedoms*), s. 7.

3   *Canada (Attorney General) v. PHS Community Services Society,* 2011 SCC 44,
     [2011] 3 S.C.R. 134.

4   *Canada (Attorney General) v. Mavi,* 2011 SCC 30, [2011] 2 S.C.R. 504.

5   *R. v. Khan,* 2001 SCC 86, [2001] 3 S.C.R. 823.

6   *R. v. Lomage; Mallet v. Administrator of the Motor Vehicle Accident Claims Act,*
     [1991] 2 O.L.R. (3d) 621.

7   Rt. Hon. Beverley McLachlin, "Legal Writing: Some Tools," quoted in *P.D. v.
     British Columbia,* 2010 BCSC 290 para. 114.

8   *Burmah Oil Co. v. Bank of England,* [1979] 1 W.L.R. 473 at 484 (Court of Appeal).

9   *Air Canada v. Secretary of State for Trade,* [1983] 2 A.C. 411.

10   *U.S. v. Cronic,* quoted in *R. v. Joanisse,* [1995] 102 C.C.C. (3d) 57.

11   William Felstiner, Richard L. Abel, and Austin Sarat, "The Emergence and
     Transformation of Disputes: Naming, Blaming, and Claiming," *Law & Society
     Review* 15, no. 3–4 (1980): 631–54.

12   *Do v. Sheffer,* 2010 ABQB 86.

13   *Use of Highway and Rules of the Road Regulation,* AR 304/2002, s. 34(1).

14 Foundation for Public Legal Education, "Legal Capability Project: Law for Everyday Life," http://www.lawforlife.org.uk/index.php/law-for-life-projects/legal-capability-for-everyday-life/.

15 "Measuring Young People's Legal Capability," Public Legal Education Network and Independent Academic Research Studies, http://www.lawforlife.org.uk/wp-content/uploads/2013/05/measuring-young-peoples-legal-capability-2009-117.pdf.

16 Lucie E. White," Subordination, Rhetorical Survival Skills, and Sunday Shoes: Notes on the Hearing of Mrs. G." *Buffalo Law Review* 38, no. 1 (1990): 1–58.

17 White, "Subordination," 58.

CHAPTER 2: LEGAL LITERACY AND OTHER LITERACIES

1 Paulo Freire and Donaldo Macedo, *Literacy: Reading the Word and the World* (London: Routledge, 1987), 9.

2 Council of Canadian Administrative Tribunals, *Literacy and Access to Administrative Justice in Canada: A Guide for the Promotion of Plain Language* (Ottawa: Council of Canadian Administrative Tribunals, 2005), 11.

3 James Boyd White, "The Invisible Discourse of the Law: Reflections on Legal Literacy and General Education," *University of Colorado Law Review* 54 (1983): 144.

4 Mary Sarah Bilder, "The Lost Lawyers: Early American Legal Literates and Transatlantic Legal Culture," *Yale Journal of Law and the Humanities* 11 (1999): 51.

5 Michael E. Manley-Casimir, Wanda M. Cassidy, and Suzanne de Castell, *Legal Literacy: Toward a Working Definition*, Report Submitted to the Canadian Law Information Council (Ottawa: Canadian Law Information Council, 1986), 47.

6 Ibid., 90; emphasis in original.

7 American Bar Association, Commission on Public Understanding about the Law, *Legal Literacy Survey Summary* (Chicago: American Bar Association, 1989), 5.

8 Canadian Bar Association, *Reading the Legal World: Literacy and Justice in Canada*, Report of the Canadian Bar Association Task Force on Legal Literacy (Ottawa: Canadian Bar Association, 1992), 23.

9 Fatema Rashid Hasan, "Limits and Possibilities of Law and Legal Literacy: Experience of Bangladesh Women," *Economic and Political Weekly* 29, no. 44 (1994): 70.

10 Irving Rootman and Deborah Gordon-El-Bihbety, *A Vision for a Health Literate Canada: Report of the Expert Panel on Health Literacy* (Ottawa: Canadian Public Health Association, 2008), 1.

11 Anna-Maria Marshall and Scott Barclay, "Introduction: In Their Own Words: How Ordinary People Construct the Legal World," *Law & Social Inquiry* 28, no. 3 (2003): 625.

12 June Louin Tapp and Felice J. Levine, "Legal Socialization: Strategies for an Ethical Legality," *Stanford Law Review* 27, no. 1 (1974): 4.

13 Ibid., 8.

14 Asian Development Bank, *Technical Assistance (Financed by the Government of the Netherlands) for Legal Literacy for Supporting Governance* (Manila: Asian Development Bank, 1999), 2.

CHAPTER 3: LEGAL STRUCTURES

1 United Nations, *Universal Declaration of Human Rights,* (1948), Art. 6.

2 *Constitution Act 1982,* [en. by the *Canada Act 1982* (UK), c. 11, s. 1] pt. I (*Canadian Charter of Rights and Freedoms*), s. 7.

3 Mather, Lynn and Barbara Yngvesson, "Language, Audience, and the Transformation of Disputes," *Law & Society Review* 15, no. 3–4 (1981): 778.

4 *Mabo and Others v. Queensland* (No. 2), [1992] HCA 23; 175 C.L.R. 1.

5 *Delgamuukw v. British Columbia,* [1997] 3 S.C.R. 1010.

6 Michel Foucault, The Archaeology of Knowledge (New York: Pantheon Books, 1973); *The Order of Things: An Archaeology of the Human Sciences* (New York: Vintage Books, 1994).

7 Jacques Derrida, *Writing and Difference,* Trans. Alan Bass (London: Routledge & Kegan Paul, 1978).

8 Peter Goodrich, "J.D.," *Cardozo Law Review* 27, no. 2 (2005): 802.

9 Anthony Giddens, *The Constitution of Society: Outline of the Theory of Structuration,* (Berkeley: University of California Press), 1984.

10 Clinton W. Francis, "Practice, Strategy and Institution: Debt Collection in the English Common-Law Courts, 1740–1840," *Northwestern University Law Review* 80 (1986): 868.

1   Susan S. Silbey, "After Legal Consciousness," *Annual Review of Law and Social Science*, 1 (2005): 323.

2   *Alberta (Child, Youth and Family Enhancement, Director) v. B.M.*, 2009 ABCA 258.

3   *R. v. Oakes*, [1986] 1 S.C.R. 103.

4   William O. Douglas, "Stare Decisis," *Columbia Law Review* 49, no. 6 (1949): 735–36.

5   Frederick F. Schauer, "Precedent," *Stanford Law Review* 39, no. 3 (1987): 577.

6   *Municipal Government Act* RSA 2000, c. M-26, s. 617.

7   Schauer, "Precedent," 601.

8   Alberta Ministry of Justice, "Alberta's Justice System and You," http://justice.alberta.ca/programs_services/public_education/Documents/ab_just_system_and_you.pdf.

9   See Rex E. Lee, "The Profession Looks at Itself—the Pound Conference of 1976," *Brigham Young University Law Review* 3 (1981): 737–40.

CHAPTER 5: LEGAL PROCESSES AND PROCEDURES

1   Ronald W. Staudt and Paula L. Hannaford, "Access to Justice for the Self-Represented Litigant: An Interdisciplinary Investigation by Designers and Lawyers," *Syracuse Law Review* 52 (2002): 1017–47.

2   Foundation for Public Legal Education, "Legal Capability Project: Law for Everyday Life," http://www.lawforlife.org.uk/index.php/law-for-life-projects/legal-capability-for-everyday-life/, 7.

3   Frank Heckman, Stuart E. Rickerson, Bruce Kauffman, and Miles Zaremski, "Legal Strategic Analysis Planning and Evaluation Control System and Method," United States Patent No. 5,875,431, http://patft.uspto.gov/netacgi/nph-Parser?Sect2=PTO1&Sect2=HITOFF&p=1&u=/netahtml/PTO/search-bool.html&r=1&f=G&l=50&d=PALL&RefSrch=yes&Query=PN/5875431; David R. Johnson, "Serving Justice with Conversational Law," *The Futurist* September-October (2012): 21–24.

4   John Thibaut and Laurens Walker, "A Theory of Procedure," *California Law Review* 66, no. 3 (1978): 541–66.

5   Tom R. Tyler, "What is Procedural Justice? Criteria Used by Citizens to Assess the Fairness of Legal Procedures," *Law & Society Review* 22, no. 1 (1988): 103–36.

6   *Constitution Act, 1982*, [en. by the *Canada Act 1982* (UK), c. 11, s. 1] pt. I (*Canadian Charter of Rights and Freedoms*), s. 7.

7   *Alberta Rules of Court.* AR 124/2010. http://www.qp.alberta.ca/documents/ rules2010/rules_vol_1.pdf. All subsequent quotations taken from this source appear in text boxes in section 5.2.

8   *Criminal Code* R.S.C., 1985, c. C-46 s. 504, http://laws-lois.justice.gc.ca/eng/ acts/C-46/. All subsequent quotations in section 5.3's text boxes are taken from this source.

9   *Criminal Code* R.S.C., 1985, c. C-46, s. 676(1)(a), http://laws-lois.justice.gc.ca/ eng/acts/C-46/page-385.html#docCont

10   Paul R. Verkuil, "A Study of Informal Adjudication Procedure," *University of Chicago Law Review* 43, no. 4 (1976): 739–96.

11   Paul R. Verkuil, "The Emerging Concept of Administrative Procedure," *Columbia Law Review* 78, no. 2 (1978): 294.

12   Alberta Law Reform Institute, *Powers and Procedures for Administrative Tribunals in Alberta* (Edmonton, AB: University of Alberta, 1999), 19–25, http://www. alri.ualberta.ca/docs/fr079.pdf.

13   David Mullan, "The Supreme Court of Canada and Tribunals—Deference to the Administrative Process: A Recent Phenomenon or a Return to Basics?" *Canadian Bar Review,* 80 (2001): 402.

14   *Administrative Procedures and Jurisdiction Act* RSA 2000, c. A-3.

15   Carla Hotel and Joan Brockman, "The Conciliatory-Adversarial Continuum in Family Law Practice," *Canadian Journal of Family Law* 12 (1994): 11–36.

16   Hotel and Brockman, "Continuum," 33.

17   Carrie Menkel-Meadow, "The Trouble with the Adversary System in a Postmodern, Multicultural World," *William and Mary Law Review* 38 (1996): 26.

18   Tom R. Tyler, "Citizen Discontent with Legal Procedures: A Social Science Perspective on Civil Procedure Reform," *American Journal of Comparative Law* 45, no. 4 (1997): 876.

19   Marc Galanter, "Why the 'Haves' Come out Ahead: Speculations on the Limits of Legal Change," *Law & Society Review* 9, no. 1 (1974): 95–160.

CHAPTER 6: LEGAL LANGUAGE

1   Aviam Soifer, "Beyond Mirrors: Lawrence Friedman's Moving Pictures," *Law & Society Review* 21 (1998): 998.

2 John M. Conley and William M. O'Barr, *Just Words: Law, Language, and Power,* 2nd ed. (Chicago: University of Chicago Press, 2005), 14.

3 Peter Goodrich, *Legal Discourse: Studies in Linguistics, Rhetoric and Legal Analysis* (New York: St Martin's Press, 1987), 206.

4 William E. Conklin, *The Phenomenology of Modern Legal Discourse: The Juridical Production and the Disclosure of Suffering* (Aldershot: Ashgate Dartmouth, 1998), 57.

5 Conley and O'Barr, *Just Words.*

6 Judith D. Fischer, "Framing Gender: Federal Appellate Judges' Choices About Gender-Neutral Language," *University of San Francisco Law Review* 43 (2009): 504.

7 *Mabo and Others v. Queensland* (No. 2), [1992] HCA 23; 175 C.L.R. 1.

8 Rudolf Flesch, "More about Gobbledygook," *Public Administration Review* 5, no. 3 (1945): 240–44.

9 George Orwell, "Politics and the English Language," https://www.mtholyoke.edu/acad/intrel/orwell46.htm.

10 Ernest Gowers, *The Complete Plain Words,* 3rd ed., rev. Sydney Greenbaum and Janet Whitcut (London: H.M.S.O., 1986).

11 Richard Darville and Gayla Reid, *Preparing Information on the Law: Guidelines for Writing, Editing and Designing* (Ottawa: Canadian Law Information Council, 1985), 24–41.

12 Darville and Reid, *Preparing Information on the Law,* 40–41.

13 Ruth Sullivan, "The Promise of Plain Language Drafting," *McGill Law Journal* 47 (2001): 20.

14 *Re. Manitoba Language Rights,* [1985] 1 S.C.R. 721.

15 Roderick A. MacDonald, "Legal Bilingualism," *McGill Law Review* 42 (1997): 22–23.

16 Jeremy Bentham, quoted in David Mellinkoff, *The Language of the Law* (Boston: Little, Brown and Company, 1963), 4.

17 Alberta. *Alberta Rules of Court,* AR 390/68, Sched. A Form E.

18 Alberta. *Alberta Rules of Court,* AR 124/2010, Sched. A Form 31.

19 Alberta. *Alberta Rules of Court,* AR 124/2010, Sched. A Form 16.

20 Mellinkoff, *Language of the Law,* 11-23.

21 Peter M. Tiersma, *Legal Language* (Chicago: University of Chicago Press, 1999), 141.

22 William J. Pencak, Ralph Lindgren, Roberta Kevelson, and Charles N. Yood, eds., *"The Law" vs. "The People:" Twelfth Round Table on Law and Semiotics* (New York: Peter Lang, 2000).

CHAPTER 7: LEGAL RESEARCH

1 Consultative Group on Research and Education in Law, *Law and Learning: Report to the Social Sciences and Humanities Research Council of Canada* quoted in Paul Chynoweth, "Legal Research," *Advanced Research Methods in the Built Environment* (Oxford: Wiley-Blackwell, 2008), 29.

2 Council of Australian Law Deans, quoted in Terry Hutchinson, "Developing Legal Research Skills: Expanding the Paradigm," *Melbourne University Law Review* 32 (2008): 1072.

3 Hutchinson, "Developing Legal Research Skills."

4 Queen's Printer, British Columbia, *Glossary*, http://www.bclaws.ca/civix/content/complete/statreg/?xsl=/templates/browse.xsl.

5 Government of Canada, Department of Justice, *Glossary*, http://laws.justice.gc.ca/eng/Glossary/.

6 Graham Garton, ed., *Canadian Charter of Rights Decisions Digest*, http://www.canlii.org/en/ca/charter_digest/index.html.

7 Canadian Law Blogs List, *Lawblogs.ca* (blog), http://www.lawblogs.ca/.

8 Judith Bannister, "Open Access to Legal Sources in Australasia: Current Debate on Crown Copyright and the Case of the Anthropomorphic Postbox," *Journal of Information, Law and Technology*, 3 (1996), http://www2.warwick.ac.uk/fac/soc/law/elj/jilt/1996_3/bannister/.

9 Graham Greenleaf, Philip Chung, and Andrew Mowbray, "Emerging Global Networks for Free Access to Law: WorldLII's Strategies 2002–2005," *Script-ed* 4, no. 4 (2007): 319–66, http://www.law.ed.ac.uk/ahrc/script-ed/vol4-4/greenleaf.pdf.

10 Teresa Scassa, "The Best Things in Law are Free?: Toward Quality Free Public Access to Primary Legal Materials in Canada," *Dalhousie Law Journal* 23, no. 2 (2000): 301–36; Janine Miller, "The Canadian Legal Information Institute—A Model for Success," *Legal Information Management* 8 no. 4 (2008): 280–82.

11 WorldLII, "Declaration on Free Access to Law," http://www.worldlii.org/worldlii/declaration/.

12 Vito Petretti, "*Matthew Bender & Co. v. West Publishing Co.*: The End of West's Legal Publishing Empire?" *Villanova Law Review* 43 (1998): 873–922.

13 *CCH Canadian Ltd. v. Law Society of Upper Canada* 2004 SCC 13, [2004] 1 S.C.R. 339.

CHAPTER 8: LEGAL INTERPRETATION

1   This example was famously used by two leading legal scholars in the course of their debate over the nature of law. See H.L.A. Hart, "Positivism and the Separation of Law and Morals," *Harvard Law Review* 71, no. 4 (1958): 593–629; Lon L. Fuller, "Positivism and Fidelity to Law—A Reply to Professor Hart," *Harvard Law Review* 71, no. 4 (1958): 630–72.

2   These examples are taken from Linda D. Jellum, "The Art of Statutory Interpretation: Identifying the Interpretive Theory of the Judges of the United States Court of Appeals for Veterans' Claims and the United States Court of Appeals for the Federal Circuit," *Louisville Law Review* 49 (2010): 59–109.

3   Hart, "Positivism," 614.

4   *Omychund v. Barker*, [1744], 1 Atk. 22, 26 E.R. 15, 22.

5   *Alberta Union of Provincial Employees v. Lethbridge Community College*, 2004 SCC 28, [2004] 1 S.C.R. 727.

6   *Interpretation Act*, R.S.A. 2000, c. I-8.

7   *Alberta Union of Provincial Employees v. Lethbridge Community College.*

8   See the discussion of Hart's views in Wil Waluchow, "Indeterminacy," *Canadian Journal of Law & Jurisprudence* 9 (1996): 397–409.

9   Ronald Dworkin, *Justice in Robes* (Cambridge, MA: Belknap Harvard, 2006).

10 *Irwin Toy Ltd. v. Québec* (Attorney General), [1989] 1 S.C.R. 927.

11 *Edwards v. A.G. of Canada*, [1928] S.C.R. 276.

12 *Edwards v. A.G. of Canada*, [1930] A.C. 124.

CHAPTER 9: LEGAL COMMUNICATION

1   Antonin Scalia and Bryan A. Garner, *Making Your Case: The Art of Persuading Judges* (Saint Paul, MN: Thomson-West, 2008), 26–28.

2   Rt. Hon. Beverley McLachlin, "Legal Writing: Some Tools," *Alberta Law Review* 39, no. 3 (2001): 700.

3   Charles J. Ten Brink, "A Jurisprudential Approach to Teaching Legal Research," *New England Law Review* 39 (2005): 307–16.

4   Brian J. Foley et al., "Teaching Students to Persuade," *Second Draft: The Bulletin of the Legal Writing Institute* 16, no. 1 (2001): 1–14; Cara Cunningham and Michelle Streicher, "The Methodology of Persuasion: A Process-based Approach to Persuasive Writing," *Legal Writing: The Journal of the Legal Writing Institute* 13 (2007): 159–98.

5   Scalia and Garner, *Making Your Case*, 178–188.

6   Rupert Haigh, *Legal English*, 3rd ed. (London: Routledge, 2012), 190–191.

7   Scalia and Garner, *Making Your Case*, 178–183.

8   Robert Barr Smith, *The Literate Lawyer: Legal Writing and Oral Advocacy*. 4th rev. ed. (Lake Mary, FL.: Vandeplas, 2009), 151–161.

9   Scalia and Garner, *Making Your Case*, 157, 161–165, 189–200.

10 *Donoghue v. Stevenson*, [1932] A.C. 562.

11 Edward H. Levi, *An Introduction to Legal Reasoning* (Chicago: University of Chicago Press, 1949).

12 Scott Brewer, "Exemplary Reasoning: Semantics, Pragmatics, and the Rational Force of Legal Argument by Analogy," *Harvard Law Review* 109, no. 5 (1996): 923–1028.

13 Frederick F. Schauer, *Thinking Like a Lawyer: A New Introduction to Legal Reasoning* (Cambridge, MA: Harvard University Press, 2009).

14 Michael Scriven, "Methods of Reasoning and Justification in Social Science and Law," *Journal of Legal Education* 23, no. 1 (1971): 189–99.

15 James F. Stratman, "The Emergence of Legal Composition as a Field of Inquiry: Evaluating the Prospects," *Review of Educational Research* 60, no. 2 (1990): 153–235.

GLOSSARY OF TERMS

A

ab initio: Latin phrase meaning "from the beginning"; if someone wants a transaction such as a contract to be reversed as if it never legally took place, they would ask that it be declared void ab initio.

Aboriginal title: In Canada, the land rights belonging to Native peoples such as First Nations and Inuit.

accept evidence: The decision made by a legal decision-maker to consider evidence as honest and reliable for the purpose of proving a fact in question.

acceptance: The act of agreeing to an offer that has been made to enter into a contract.

access to justice: Capacity to make use of the legal system to pursue legal rights.

accused: Person charged with a crime.

action: Legal proceeding in court.

activist: Used to describe judges who use policy in addition to law as a basis for decision-making.

Acts: Another name for legislation; statutes.

address for service: Place designated by a party where notices concerning legal proceedings may be sent to them.

adjournment: Interruption of a hearing to be continued at a later time.

administrative boards (or administrative tribunals): Bodies created by government to make quasi-judicial decisions.

administrative law: Branch of law concerning the basic legal principles to be followed by administrative tribunals under the supervision of the courts.

admissibility of evidence: Criteria to be met to allow information to become evidence in a legal proceeding.

admit evidence: Act of a legal decision-maker to allow information to be considered as evidence.

alternative dispute resolution (ADR): A variety of more informal methods for resolving disputes instead of a trial, including mediation and conciliation.

adversarial system: Legal proceedings guided by the parties in dispute.

adversarialism: Climate of competition and distrust found in the adversarial system.

affidavit: Sworn (or affirmed) written record of information provided by a person.

affirmation: Non-religious alternative to swearing an oath.

allegations: Version of facts put forward by a party.

amendments: Change to a document or legislation.

analogical reasoning: Using analogy to link different cases as a guide to decision-making.

annotated statutes: Version of legislation incorporating references to cases in which it has been mentioned.

appeal: Act of requesting reversal or change in a judgment that has been made.

appeal court (or appellate court): Court with jurisdiction to hear appeals from judgments of lower courts.

appellant: Party who appeals.

application of law: Decision about how the law governs the facts that have been proved, and the result to which it leads.

applied research: Research intended to help solve practical problems.

arbitration: Form of binding dispute resolution by a non-judicial person appointed by the parties.

argument: Persuasive reasoning about the facts or law presented to a legal decision-maker.

assignment: Legal act of substituting a new party in a contract.

attorney: In the US, a lawyer.

authorities: Legal sources such as cases and legislation used to support argument.

B

bailiff: Officer of a court often engaged in enforcement.

balance of probabilities: Standard of proof required in civil proceedings; more probable than not.

balancing (legal principles):
Act of considering the relative importance of competing principles in reaching a legal decision.

Bar: A word used to refer to lawyers, often in a particular jurisdiction such as a city or a Province. It is derived from the bar used in courtrooms to separate the public from officers of the court.

Bench: A word used to refer to judges hearing a case or all judges in a particular jurisdiction. It is derived from the old courtroom setting in which presiding judges sat on a bench.

beyond a reasonable doubt:
Standard of proof required in criminal proceedings; no real doubt about the facts.

binding authority: Legal authority that must be followed by the decision-maker.

binding decision: Decision that parties must comply with.

binding precedent: Case authority that must be followed by the decision-maker.

black-letter law: Rules and legislation forming part of the law.

boilerplate: Traditional standard wording in contracts.

breach of contract: Failing to meet contractual obligations.

briefs: In the US, written submissions or written argument.

burden (or onus) of proof:
Responsibility to provide evidence to prove facts.

C

canon law: Law applying to members of a church, such as the Roman Catholic Church.

canons of construction: Rules for interpretation of law.

case citation: Reference information for locating the text of a reported case.

case synthesis: Act of drawing common ideas or principles out of a series of reported cases.

catchwords (or keywords): Legal terms identifying the issues considered in a reported case.

cautions: Advice on legal rights given by police to suspects.

certiorari: Legal process to allow a court to review the decision of an administrative tribunal.

cestui que trust: Person for whose benefit a trust is created.

Chapter: Title given to a single statute forming part of the legislation in a jurisdiction.

charge: The offence alleged to have been committed by an accused.

citator (case citator; statute citator): Publication recording where cases or statutes have been mentioned in other cases.

cite a case: Refer to a reported case as an authority.

cited for contempt: Summoned to appear before the court to answer a charge of contempt.

citing from authority: Refer to legal authorities to support an argument.

civil cases: Legal proceedings of all types, excluding criminal cases.

civil codes: Name for legislation in civil law jurisdictions.

civil law: Usually used to describe the law in European jurisdictions and those that are based on such models.

civil litigation (or civil proceedings): Legal proceedings in civil (non-criminal) matters.

civil process and procedure: Process and procedure in civil (non-criminal) matters.

claimant: In the UK, the plaintiff.

Clarity International: International organization promoting clear language in business and government.

clause (of legislation): Structural component of a section or subsection of legislation.

collaborative law: Type of practice used by lawyers who agree to negotiate instead of going court.

commission: Another name for an administrative body which may make quasi-judicial decisions.

common law: Body of law based on case precedents.

common law rules or principles: General rules or principles derived from a synthesis of the results of a series of similar cases.

comprehensive publishing policy: Policy of reporting all written judgments in a jurisdiction.

conciliation: Form of alternative dispute resolution in which the conciliator may suggest solutions.

concur: Judge's act of agreeing with a judgment written by another judge.

conflict of facts: Dispute over what happened.

conflict of interests: Dispute arising out of people's basic needs and desires (their interests) which are perceived to conflict.

consideration: Something of value given to create a contract.

consistency: Principle used by administrative tribunals when deciding similar cases.

constitution: The highest law in a jurisdiction that governs other laws.

contempt citation: Document summoning a person to court to answer a charge of contempt.

contempt of court: Acting in disrespect of the court or its orders.

contextual legal research: Research that takes into account the social context of law.

contra proferentem: Latin term meaning "against the one who presents something"; principle used in interpreting contracts written solely by one party.

contract: Binding legal agreement.

contracts of adhesion: Contracts written by one party with no input from other contracting parties.

cooperative law: Type of legal practice similar to collaborative law.

core meaning: Undisputed legal meaning of a word or phrase.

courts martial: Courts established to govern military personnel.

credibility: Test of whether the evidence given by a witness should be accepted as honest and dependable.

criminal proceedings: Legal proceedings involving an accused charged with an offence.

criminal process and procedure: Process and procedure in criminal proceedings.

cross examination: Questioning of a witness by an opposing party.

Crown: Used to describe the head of state and the state itself in a constitutional monarchy such as Canada.

crown copyright: The government's right to prevent the use of documents created by government officials.

D

damages: Compensation for harm paid by a person found legally responsible for causing it.

deconstruction: Interpretive technique revealing the indefiniteness of the meaning of a text.

deductive reasoning: Logical reasoning from one true statement to another.

defamation: Tort committed by someone who harms the reputation of another.

defendant: Person who is sued in civil proceedings.

demand for (or of) notice: Request to be notified of steps taken in legal proceedings.

disclosure: Revealing information before a trial or other hearing occurs.

discovery: Legal term for disclosure.

discretion: Power to make a decision within a range of possibilities.

discretion according to law: Power to make a decision within a range of possibilities while taking legal rules and principles into account.

dispute resolution: Termination of a dispute.

dissenting judgment: Judgment given by a judge who does not agree with the majority of judges who heard the case.

distinguish: Act of pointing out dissimilarities between two cases for the purpose of showing that one is not a precedent for the other.

division (of legislation): Smaller component of a part of legislation.

doctrinal legal research: Research for the purpose of arguing legal issues or clarifying the law.

doctrine of precedent: Principle that like cases should be decided in the same way.

documentary evidence: Information in the form of documents presented as evidence.

drug courts: Special courts intended to deal with drug offences with rehabilitation of offenders in mind.

E

economics and law: Type of legal studies using economic principles and techniques to analyze law and legal processes.

elements (of a tort): All of the components that must be proved to find a person responsible for harm.

en banc: All the judges of a court sitting together to hear a case.

environmental literacy: Understanding of the interrelation of society and the environment.

estate: The type of rights held over land, or, the property left by a deceased person.

estoppel: Principle preventing someone from denying something they have said that has been relied on by another.

evidence: Information admitted by a legal decision maker to help prove the facts.

ex parte: Latin phrase for "without the other party"; something that happens without all parties to a dispute being present.

examination for discovery: In Canada, oral questioning of an opposing party before trial as part of disclosure.

examine: Question a witness.

exclusion (or exemption) clause: Part of contract protecting one party from legal responsibility.

executive branch or institution: Part of government which administers the law.

exemplary reasoning: Legal reasoning using examples by way of analogy.

expert opinion: Opinion about the facts given by a person recognized as an expert in their field.

expert witness: Witness accepted by a legal decision maker as being an expert in a particular field.

external perspective: Perspective on law from outside the legal system.

federal states: Nation-states with several equal internal legal jurisdictions.

financial literacy: Understanding of the economics of daily life.

finding of fact: Decision-maker's conclusion that a fact has been sufficiently proved.

finding of law: Decision-maker's conclusion about the relevancy, meaning, or application of a law.

form of address: Respectful words used when speaking to a judge or other legal decision. maker.

formal judgment: Document that orders action based on a legal decision.

forum: Court or tribunal.

framing: Describing an event or situation using legal concepts and terminology for the purpose of presenting a legal issue.

fundamental justice: The basic principles of fairness to be followed by every legal decision-maker.

F

factual argument: Argument about the proof of facts through evidence.

factum: Name given to written argument in some courts.

G

gender-neutral: Language that does not refer to a single gender.

gobbledygook: Name given to wordy and unclear government documents.

guardian ad litem: Adult person appointed to represent a child in legal proceedings.

H

habeas corpus: Latin phrase for "custody of the person," used when courts review the legality of an individual's detention.

headnote: A brief summary of the legal issues and decisions in a reported case.

health literacy: Understanding of the interrelation of health and ordinary life.

hearing: Opportunity for disputing parties to present evidence and make arguments.

hearsay: Second-hand evidence given by someone who heard it from another.

hearsay rule: Rule of evidence law preventing hearsay from being admitted, with some exceptions.

hermeneutic tradition: Interpretation of texts to discover the true meaning of them.

holding: Conclusion of legal decision-maker.

homeostasis: Tendency of a system to preserve equilibrium.

I

inadmissible: Description of information that may not admitted as evidence.

incorporation by reference: Inclusion of one text within another by reference to another document.

indeterminacy: Unpredictability of a result.

indictment: Formal document used to charge an accused person.

inductive reasoning: Legal reasoning from specific examples toward a general principle.

inferences: Facts found to be true through proof of other facts.

information: Formal document used to bring an accused before a criminal court.

information literacy: Understanding of how to access and evaluate publicly available information.

inquisitorial system: Legal proceedings guided by the decision-maker instead of the parties.

instructions: A client's wishes provided to a lawyer.

intention (of legislators): The problem lawmakers had in mind to solve through legislation.

interlocutory: Something that occurs after legal proceedings have been commenced and before trial.

intermediate courts: Courts that hear appeals from lower courts and from which appeals may be taken to higher courts.

internal perspective: Perspective on the law taken by someone operating within the legal system.

interpretive argument: Argument about the proper interpretation of law.

intervener: Person allowed to take part in proceedings between others.

intoxicated persons: Category of people who may be treated differently for some legal purposes, such as contracting with others.

J

judgment debtor and judgment creditor: A person who owes money according to the order of a court, and the person to whom it is owed.

judgments: Decision of a judge, usually accompanied by the reasons for making it.

judicial branch or institution: Part of government with a judicial role.

judicial dispute resolution or judicial settlement conferencing: Informal resolution of a case by a judge without a trial.

judicial interference: Criticism levelled at judges who interpret legislation in a way contrary to the expectations of lawmakers.

judicial law-making: Description of the activity of judges who interpret legislation in a way contrary to the expectations of lawmakers.

judicial notice (of fact and of law): Finding a fact or law to be proved without evidence being given.

judicial review: Court process to examine the decision of an administrative tribunal.

jurilinguists: Experts in legal expression in two or more languages.

jurisdiction: Authority of a given court or tribunal over persons or legal matters.

jurisprudence: Case law interpreting legislation; also legal philosophy.

justiciable: Capable of being decided by a court.

L

language rights: Rights to use a particular language in legal matters and proceedings.

law and psychology: Type of legal studies that examines law and legal systems using psychological theory and techniques.

law and society: Name given to legal studies that focus on the interrelationship of law and society.

law dictionaries: Dictionaries containing definitions of legal terms and phrases.

Law French: Archaic form of French still found in some legal terms and phrases.

law in context: Name given to legal studies that focus on the interrelationship of law and society.

law journals: Serial publications containing scholarly articles about law and the legal system.

law of evidence: Law that governs the admissibility and use of evidence in hearings.

law reform: Research and study for the purpose of improving existing law.

law reviews: Another name for law journals.

leading cases: Select cases published and used to guide decision-making.

legal aid: Government assistance for hiring lawyers.

legal bilingualism: Principle that when law is expressed in two languages, both versions should be treated equally and should convey the same meaning.

legal capability: Ability to make use of the law to achieve legal goals.

legal case analysis: Analysis for the purpose of determining a reported case's value as a precedent.

legal characterization or categorization: Another name for framing.

legal citation: System for referencing legal authorities.

legal consciousness: Ideas and attitudes about law prevalent in society.

legal digest: Publication containing summaries of cases arranged by subject matter.

legal discourse: Communication among people who work within a legal system.

legal duty: Duty to act or to refrain from interfering with others imposed by law.

legal encyclopedia: Publication containing summaries of legal rules, principles, cases, and legislation arranged by subject matter.

legal interpretation: Process of reading and giving meaning to legal texts.

legal issue: Question framed in legal terms to be decided by a decision-maker.

legal liability: Responsibility for harm imposed by law.

legal mobilization: Using law to accomplish one's goals.

legal obligation: Responsibility to act or to refrain from acting imposed by law.

legal person: Entity recognized as having legal rights and responsibilities.

legal pluralism: Coexistence of two or more legal systems in a geographic area.

legal principles: General guides to legal decision-making that are not part of legislation.

legal profession: Practising lawyers.

legal rights: Power to do something given by law.

legal socialization: Becoming familiar with legal traditions and adept at legal practices.

legal system: The interconnected institutions in society concerned with judging and enforcing law.

legal terminology: Unique words and phrases used within legal discourse.

legal treatises: Scholarly books about legal subjects.

legalese: Unique terminology used within legal discourse.

legislation: Written law made by legislative bodies.

legislative branch or institution: Lawmaking branch of government.

legislative drafting: Designing and writing legislation.

legislative interpretation: Reading and giving meaning to legislation.

legitimacy: Being accepted as fit and proper to carry out a function in society.

licensing agreements: In relation to copyright, allowing someone else to republish material.

literal meaning rule: Rule of legal interpretation that only takes account of the exact words that have been used without regard for other considerations.

litigant: Person who is a party to legal proceedings.

litigation: Legal proceedings for the resolution of a dispute.

litigious: Using litigation as the preferred method to resolve disputes.

loose parts: Recently passed legislation not yet bound in a volume.

M

managerial judging: Active intervention by a judge in the progress of litigation.

mandamus: Court process for controlling administrative action.

martial law: Law applicable to military personnel.

med-arb: Dispute resolution process providing for mediation followed by arbitration if necessary.

media literacy: Understanding the interrelation of mass media and everyday life.

mediation: Alternative dispute resolution process guided by a mediator.

meeting of minds: Agreement on reciprocal rights and obligations in the process of entering into a contract.

mens rea: Latin phrase meaning "having the thing in mind," which describes a mental state of intention to do an act or achieve a result required in criminal law.

mentally incompetent persons: Category of persons treated differently for the purpose of entering into contracts and in other legal situations.

merits: The substantive legal issues to be decided as contrasted with procedural matters.

minor persons: People who have not yet reached the age of being able to act legally for themselves; people under the "age of majority."

modern principle (or method) of interpretation: In Canada, the method of interpretation described by Professor Driedger and approved by the Supreme Court of Canada.

mortgage: Creditor's claim over land.

N

Native title: In Australia, the land rights belonging to the Aboriginal people.

natural justice: Basic principles of fairness when conducting a hearing.

negligence: Tort based on causing harm to another.

neighbour principle: Criterion used to decide whether a tort has been committed by one person against another.

neutral citation: Case citation provided by the court issuing the judgment.

normative expectations: Belief that others will act in a way that is generally approved in society.

noteup: Bringing a reported case or piece of legislation up to date with later cases or amendments.

numeracy: Understanding of and skill with using mathematics.

O

oath: Religious promise to tell the truth.

obiter dicta (or just obiter or dicta): Latin phrase meaning comments by a judge that are not part of the reasoning leading to a decision.

object (of an Act): The result expected from applying and enforcing legislation.

offer: Proposal to enter into a contract that may be agreed to through acceptance.

officialese: Jargon used by administrative officials.

one-shotters: Parties who experience litigation only one time.

open access: Free access to the public

operative: Legal wording which accomplishes a goal such as a gift.

opinions: In the US, the reasons for decision given by judges.

oral argument (or oral submissions): Oral presentations to a legal decision-maker about the facts and law in a case.

oral judgment: Decision given by a judge orally.

order of the court: Document embodying a judge's direction.

ordinary witness: Person who is not an expert who gives testimony based on their own personal knowledge.

originalism: Method of legal interpretation that tries to carry out the intention of the lawmakers who originally passed legislation.

overrule: Reverse a judgment made by a lower court.

oyez: Latin for "Hear" announced at the beginning of hearings of the Supreme Court in the US.

P

panel: A group of judges hearing a case.

parallel citation: Legal reference giving several alternative sources.

parol evidence rule: Rule of evidence that oral agreements can't change written ones.

part (of legislation): Largest component into which legislation is divided.

particulars: Details of a claim or defence provided to avoid surprise.

parties: Persons pursuing or defending legal proceedings.

penumbra: Meaning of a word or phrase that is uncertain and disputed.

plain (legal) language: Clear language that avoids legalese and is readily understandable by the average person.

plain English: Clear language that avoids jargon and is readily understandable by the average person.

plaintiff: Person who commences civil proceedings.

plea: Answer to a charge made by an accused person.

pleading: Written statement of legal claims or defences.

point in time searching: Facility to discover the wording of legislation at a precise point in time.

policy: Guide to legal decision-making in addition to legal authority.

post-structuralism: Name given to theories and techniques for analyzing and understanding people and society which do not privilege institutions and other cultural constructions but instead emphasize human freedom to act.

precedent: Similar reported case that guides legal decision-making to the same result.

predictive reasoning: Legal argument about the probable consequences of a particular decision.

preliminary inquiry: Discretionary step in criminal proceedings.

primary legal materials: Reported cases and published statutes.

principles of legal interpretation: General guides to interpretation less specific than rules.

principles of natural justice: Basic requirements of fairness in a hearing.

privilege: Right to keep a communication private, such as that between a lawyer and their client.

pro bono (publico): Latin "for the good (of the public)," description of legal services provided free of charge in the public interest.

pro se: Latin for "for oneself"; litigant without a lawyer.

problem-solving courts: Courts intended to address community issues in addition to individual criminal offences.

procedural justice: Experience of being treated fairly and respectfully in legal proceedings regardless of the outcome.

procedural steps: Actions required to be taken by the parties in legal proceedings.

process: Document used in legal proceedings required to be delivered to other parties.

process server: Person who delivers documents required in legal proceedings.

prosecutor: Person representing the state in criminal proceedings.

public domain: Freely accessible by the public.

pure research: Research intended to add to knowledge for its own sake.

Q

quasi-judicial: Description of administrative tribunals that make decisions affecting people's legal rights and responsibilities.

Queen: The word used to describe the sovereign in constitutional monarchies such as Canada.

Queen's Printer: Official publisher of government documents.

R

radiating effect: Influence of court decisions on people in similar situations.

ratio decidendi (or ratio): Latin for "reasons for decision" given by a judge to justify the result.

Regina: Latin for "Queen"; used in the title of criminal cases.

regulations: Subsidiary legislation made under the authority of an act.

reifying: Effect of giving apparent substance to an otherwise abstract and insubstantial concept.

relational contracts: Contracts intended to operate over many years, thus creating an ongoing relationship between the parties.

relevance: Criterion for determining which facts and evidence should be considered in a hearing based upon the law to be applied.

remedy (or relief): Action requested to be ordered by the court.

repeal: Act of removing legislation as part of existing law in force.

repeat players: Description of litigants who are often in court.

reply (or rebuttal): Response to the evidence or argument made by an opposing side in litigation.

reporter or report series: Serial publication containing court decisions in chronological order.

reserved (judgment or decision): Judgment given after the close of a hearing.

respondent: Person opposing an appeal or an application to the court.

restorative justice: Principle that justice should promote healing.

retroactive effect: New legislation that applies to events in the past.

revised statutes: Collection of all statutes brought up to date with amendments as at a certain date.

rhetorical: Description of communication that is meant to persuade.

rhetorical tradition: Approach to legal communication which emphasizes its persuasive nature.

right to be heard: One of the principles of natural justice requiring a decision-maker to consider argument and evidence presented by a party.

rule of law: The principle that all citizens are subject to and equal before the law, which the government must obey as well.

rules of court: Rules of procedure adopted by a particular court.

S

scheme (of an Act): General design of legislation to accomplish its purpose.

scope (of law): Range of factual situations governed by a particular law.

section (of legislation): Basic structural component of legislation expressed as a sentence.

selective publishing policy: Policy of only publishing leading cases that are considered important to the development of the law.

self-determination: Right to decide one's actions without interference.

self-government: Right to make laws without interference.

self-represented: Litigant without a lawyer.

separation of powers: Allocation of different functions among the branches of government.

service of process: Delivering a legal document to a person.

settlement: Agreement to resolve a dispute and terminate litigation without a trial.

shadow of the law: Expression used to describe the radiating effect of legal decisions on others.

Sharia law: Traditional Muslim law.

socio-legal: Type of legal studies focusing on the interrelation of law and society.

sociology of law: Legal studies using sociological theory.

sovereign: The constitutional monarch in nations such as Canada.

standard forms: Identical contracts and other documents used regularly in a particular business.

standard of proof: Degree of certainty required to prove a fact.

standard of review: Criterion used to decide whether a court will reverse a decision of an administrative tribunal.

standards (or tests): Criteria developed by case law to guide legal decision-making.

state: The government considered as a legal person.

statement of case: In the UK, a statement of claim.

Statement of Claim: In Canada, the document containing claims made by a plaintiff.

Statement of Defence: In Canada, the document containing defences raised by a defendant.

statute: Legislation passed by a lawmaking body such as a Parliament.

statute book: All of the legislation in force in a particular jurisdiction.

statutory (or legislative) definitions: Definitions of words or phrases contained in legislation that must be used when interpreting it.

statutory construction: Another name for legislative interpretation.

statutory instrument: A document having the force and effect of legislation although not passed by a legislative body.

statutory interpretation: Another name for legislative interpretation.

structuralism: Approaches to analysing and understanding people and society according to social structures such as institutions and other cultural constructions that fulfill functional roles.

structuration: Giddens' idea that social structures both constrain and empower human action.

style of cause: Heading of documents in litigation giving the parties' names.

subclause (of legislation): Smallest structural component of legislation.

submissions: Arguments of fact and law made to a legal decision-maker.

subsection (of legislation): Structural component of legislation into which a section may be divided.

summons (summonsed): Document ordering a person to appear in court.

superior and inferior courts: Courts with unlimited jurisdiction and those with limits on their jurisdiction.

syllogism: Logical statement composed of a major and minor premise followed by a conclusion.

T

terms of art: Words with a special meaning in a particular context.

terra nullius: Latin for "nobody's country"; the legal principle overturned when courts recognized native title in Australia.

territorial sovereignty: The right to exercise legal jurisdiction over a particular geographical area.

testify: Give oral evidence in a hearing.

testimony: Evidence given by a witness in a hearing.

textualism: Approach to legal interpretation that emphasizes the words used over all other considerations.

therapeutic jurisprudence: Principle that justice should heal, not harm.

third party: Additional party in litigation who is not plaintiff or defendant; also an impartial person who helps to resolve a dispute between others.

tort: Harm recognized in common law for which a claim for compensation may be made against the party who caused it.

transactional: Description of an interaction or communication for the purpose of exchange rather than dispute.

trial: Oral hearing leading to judgment.

trial by ambush: Being surprised at trial by evidence that was not disclosed beforehand.

trial judge: Judge who presides over a trial.

tribunals, boards, and commissions: Names for administrative bodies that may be authorized to make quasi-judicial decisions.

U

unenforceable: Contract or other agreement that will not be enforced by the courts.

unfettered discretion: Authority to make a decision without regard for legal rules and principles.

V

venue: Location of a hearing.

victim (impact) statements: Information provided to a court by victims for the purpose of helping to determine the proper punishment to be imposed on a convicted criminal.

viva voce: Latin for "live voice"; description of testimony given by a witness orally and in person.

voir dire: Old French and Latin term for a special hearing to decide whether evidence is admissible.

W

weigh evidence: Act of deciding whether evidence is sufficient to prove a fact according to the relevant standard of proof.

witness: Person who provides information as evidence in a hearing.

written submissions (or written argument): Document containing arguments of law or fact submitted to a legal decision-maker.

BIBLIOGRAPHY

CASES

Air Canada v. Secretary of State for Trade, [1983] House of Lords, 2 A.C. 394.

Alberta (Child, Youth and Family Enhancement, Director) v. B.M., 2009 ABCA 258.

Alberta Union of Provincial Employees v. Lethbridge Community College, 2004 SCC28, [2004] 1 S.C.R 727.

Burmah Oil Co. v. Bank of England, [1979] 1 W.L.R. 473 (Court of Appeal).

Canada (Attorney General) v. Mavi, 2011 SCC 30, [2011] 2 S.C.R. 504.

Canada (Attorney General) v. PHS Community Services Society, 2011 SCC 44, [2011] 3 S.C.R. 134.

CCH Canadian Ltd. v. Law Society of Upper Canada, 2004 SCC 13, [2004] 1 S.C.R. 339.

Delgamuukw v. British Columbia, [1997] 3 S.C.R. 1010.

Do v. Sheffer, 2010 ABQB 86.

Donoghue v. Stevenson, [1932] A.C. 562.

Edwards v. A.G. of Canada, [1928] S.C.R. 276.

Edwards v. A.G. of Canada, [1930] A.C. 124.

Irwin Toy Ltd. v. Quebec (Attorney General), [1989] 1 S.C.R. 927.

Mabo and Others v. Queensland (No. 2), [1992] HCA 23, 1 C.L.R. 175.

Omychund v. Barker, [1744] 1 Atk. 22, 26 E.R. 15.

P.D. v. British Columbia, 2010 BCSC 290.

R. v. Khan,2001 SCC 86, [2001] 3 S.C.R. 823.

R. v. Lomage; Mallet v. Administrator of the Motor Vehicle Accident Claims Act, [1991] 2 O.R. (3d) 621.

R. v. Oakes, [1986] 1 S.C.R. 103.

Re. Manitoba Language Rights, [1985] 1 S.C.R. 721.

U.S. v. Cronic, -(1984) 104 S. Ct. 2039 per Stevens J. at 2045 (United States Supreme Court),quoted in *R. v. Joanisse* [1995] 102 C.C.C. (3d) 35.

GOVERNMENT DOCUMENTS

Alberta Ministry of Justice. "Alberta's Justice System and You." http://justice. alberta.ca/programs_services/public_education/Documents/ab_just_system_ and_you.pdf.

Government of Canada, Department of Justice. *Glossary*. http://laws.justice.gc.ca/ eng/Glossary/.

Queen's Printer, British Columbia. *Glossary*. http://www.bclaws.ca/civix/ content/complete/statreg/?xsl=/templates/browse.xsl.

LEGISLATION

Alberta. *Administrative Procedures and Jurisdiction Act of Alberta*. R.S.A. 2000, c. A-3.

Alberta. *Alberta Rules of Court*. AR 124/2010. http://www.qp.alberta.ca/ documents/rules2010/rules_vol_1.pdf.

Alberta. *Interpretation Act*. R.S.A. 2000, c. I-8.

Alberta. *Municipal Government Act*. R.S.A. 2000 s. 617, c. M-26.

Alberta. *Use of Highway and Rules of the Road Regulation*. AR304/2002.

Canada. *Criminal Code*. R.S.C., 1985, c. C-46. http://laws-lois.justice.gc.ca/eng/ acts/C-46/.

Canada. *Constitution Act, 1982*, [en. by the *Canada Act* 1982 (UK), c. 11, s. 1] pt. I (Canadian Charter of Rights and Freedoms), s. 7.

United Nations. 1948. *Universal Declaration of Human Rights*.

SECONDARY SOURCES

American Bar Association, Commission on Public Understanding about the Law. Legal Literacy Survey Summary. Chicago: American Bar Association, 1989.

Asian Development Bank. Technical Assistance (Financed by the Government of the Netherlands) for Legal Literacy for Supporting Governance. Manila: Asian Development Bank, 1999.

Alberta Law Reform Institute. *Powers and Procedures for Administrative Tribunals in Alberta*. Edmonton, AB: University of Alberta, 1999. http://www.alri.ualberta.ca/docs/fr079.pdf.

Bannister, Judith. "Open Access to Legal Sources in Australasia: Current Debate on Crown Copyright and the Case of the Anthropomorphic Postbox." *Journal of Information, Law and Technology* 3 (1996). http://www2.warwick.ac.uk/fac/soc/law/elj/jilt/1996_3/bannister/.

Bilder, Mary Sarah. "The Lost Lawyers: Early American Legal Literates and Transatlantic Legal Culture." *Yale Journal of Law and the Humanities* 11 (1999): 47–112.

Brewer, Scott. "Exemplary Reasoning: Semantics, Pragmatics, and the Rational Force of Legal Argument by Analogy." *Harvard Law Review* 109, no. 5 (1996): 923–1028.

Canadian Bar Association. *Reading the Legal World: Literacy and Justice in Canada*. Report of the Canadian Bar Association Task Force on Legal Literacy. Ottawa: Author, 1992.

Chynoweth, Paul. "Legal Research." Chapter 3 in *Advanced Research Methods in the Built Environment*, edited by Andrew Knight and Less Ruddock, 28–38. Oxford: Wiley-Blackwell, 2008.

Conklin, William E. *The Phenomenology of Modern Legal Discourse: The Juridical Production and the Disclosure of Suffering*. Aldershot: Ashgate Dartmouth, 1998.

Conley, John M., and William M. O'Barr. *Just Words: Law, Language, and Power*. 2nd ed. Chicago: University of Chicago Press, 2005.

Council of Canadian Administrative Tribunals. *Literacy and Access to Administrative Justice in Canada: A Guide for the Promotion of Plain Language*. Ottawa: Author, 2005. http://www.ccat-ctac.org/en/pdfs/literacy/Literacyandjustice.pdf.

Cunningham, Cara, and Michelle Streicher. "The Methodology of Persuasion: A Process-Based Approach to Persuasive Writing." *Legal Writing: The Journal of the Legal Writing Institute* 13 (2007): 159–98.

Darville, Richard, and Gayla Reid. *Preparing Information on the Law: Guidelines for Writing, Editing and Designing*. Ottawa: Canadian Law Information Council, 1985.

Derrida, Jacques. *Writing and Difference*. Trans. Alan Bass. London: Routledge & Kegan Paul, 1978.

Douglas, William O. "Stare Decisis." *Columbia Law Review* 49, no. 6 (1949): 735–58.

Dworkin, Ronald. *Justice in Robes*. Cambridge, MA: Belknap Harvard, 2006.

Felstiner, William L. F., Richard L. Abel, and Austin Sarat. "The Emergence and Transformation of Disputes: Naming, Blaming, Claiming." *Law & Society Review* 15, no. 3–4 (1980): 631–54.

Fischer, Judith D. "Framing Gender: Federal Appellate Judges' Choices About Gender-Neutral Language." *University of San Francisco Law Review* 43 (2009): 473–506.

Flesch, Rudolf. "More about Gobbledygook." *Public Administration Review* 5, no. 3 (1945): 240–44.

Foley, Brian J., Susan Hanley Kosse, Sue Liemer, Sheila Simon, Myra G. Orlen, Ruth Anne Robbins, Patricia A. Legge, James P. Eyster, Sharon Pocock, Ken Swift, Sophie Sparrow, Clifford S. Zimmerman, and Nancy Soonpaa. "Teaching Students to Persuade." *Second Draft, The Bulletin of the Legal Writing Institute* 16, no. 1 (2001): 1–14.

Foucault, Michel. *The Archaeology of Knowledge*. Trans. A.M. Sheridan Smith. New York: Pantheon Books, 1973.

——. *The Order of Things: An Archaeology of the Human Sciences*. New York: Vintage Books, 1994.

Foundation for Public Legal Education. "Legal Capability Project: Law for Everyday Life." http://www.lawforlife.org.uk/law-for-life-projects/legal-capability-project-law-for-everyday-life,10258,FP.html.

Francis, Clinton W. "Practice, Strategy and Institution: Debt Collection in the English Common-Law Courts, 1740–1840." *Northwestern University Law Review* 80 (1986): 807–940.

Freire, Paulo, and Donaldo Macedo. *Literacy: Reading the Word & the World*. London: Routledge, 1987.

Fuller, Lon L. "Positivism and Fidelity to Law – A Reply to Professor Hart." *Harvard Law Review* 71, no. 4 (1958): 630–72.

Galanter, Marc. "Why the 'Haves' Come Out Ahead: Speculations on the Limits of Legal Change." *Law & Society Review* 9, no. 1 (1974): 95–160.

Garton, Graham, ed. "Canadian Charter of Rights Decisions Digest." http://www.canlii.org/en/ca/charter_digest/index.html.

Giddens, Anthony. *The Constitution of Society: Outline of the Theory of Structuration*. Berkeley: University of California Press, 1984.

Goodrich, Peter. "J.D." *Cardozo Law Review* 27, no. 2 (2005): 801–14.

——. *Legal Discourse: Studies in Linguistics, Rhetoric and Legal Analysis*. New York: St Martin's Press, 1987.

Gowers, Ernest. *The Complete Plain Words.* 3rd ed. Rev. Sydney Greenbaum and Janet Whitcut. London: H.M.S.O., 1986.

Greenleaf, Graham, Philip Chung, and Andrew Mowbray. "Emerging Global Networks for Free Access to Law: WorldLII's Strategies 2002–2005." *Scripted.* 4, no. 4 (2007): 319–66. http://www.law.ed.ac.uk/ahrc/script-ed/vol4-4/greenleaf.pdf.

Haigh, Rupert. *Legal English.* 3rd ed. London: Routledge, 2012.

Hart, H.L.A. "Positivism and the Separation of Law and Morals." *Harvard Law Review* 71, no. 4 (1958): 593–629.

Hasan, Fatema Rashid. "Limits and Possibilities of Law and Legal Literacy: Experience of Bangladesh Women." *Economic and Political Weekly* 29, no. 44 (1994): 69–76.

Heckman, Frank, Stuart E. Rickerson, Bruce Kauffman, and Miles Zaremski. "Legal Strategic Analysis Planning and Evaluation Control System and Method." United States Patent No. 5,875,431. http://patft.uspto.gov/netacgi/nph-Parser?Sect2=PTO1&Sect2=HITOFF&p=1&u=/netahtml/PTO/search-bool.html&r=1&f=G&l=50&d=PALL&RefSrch=yes&Query=PN/5875431.

Hotel, Carla, and Joan Brockman. "The Conciliatory-Adversarial Continuum in Family Law Practice." *Canadian Journal of Family Law* 12 (1994): 11–36.

Hutchinson, Terry. "Developing Legal Research Skills: Expanding the Paradigm." *Melbourne University Law Review* 32 (2008): 1065–1095.

Jellum, Linda D. "The Art of Statutory Interpretation: Identifying the Interpretive Theory of the Judges of the United States Court of Appeals for Veterans' Claims and the United States Court of Appeals for the Federal Circuit." *Louisville Law Review* 49 (2010): 59–109.

Johnson, David R. "Serving Justice with Conversational Law." *The Futurist* September-October 2012: 21–24.

Lee, Rex E. "The Profession Looks at Itself—The Pound Conference of 1976." *Brigham Young University Law Review* 3 (1981): 737–40.

Levi, Edward H. *An Introduction to Legal Reasoning.* Chicago: University of Chicago Press, 1949.

Llewellyn, Karl N. "Remarks on the Theory of Appellate Decision and The Rules or Canons About How Statutes are to be Construed." *Vanderbilt Law Review* 3 (1950): 395–406.

MacDonald, Roderick A. "Legal Bilingualism." *McGill Law Review* 42 (1997): 119–65.

Manley-Casimir, Michael E., Wanda M. Cassidy, and Suzanne de Castell. *Legal Literacy: Towards a Working Definition*. Report Submitted to the Canadian Law Information Council. Ottawa: Canadian Law Information Council, 1986.

Marshall, Anna-Maria, and Scott Barclay. "Introduction: In Their Own Words: How Ordinary People Construct the Legal World." *Law & Social Inquiry* 28, no. 3 (2003): 617–28.

Mather, Lynn, and Barbara Yngvesson. "Language, Audience, and the Transformation of Disputes." *Law & Society Review* 15, no. 3–4 (1981): 775–821.

McLachlin, Rt. Hon. Beverley. "Legal Writing: Some Tools." *Alberta Law Review* 39, no. 3 (2001): 695–702.

Mellinkoff, David. *The Language of the Law*. Boston: Little, Brown and Company, 1963.

Menkel-Meadow, Carrie. "The Trouble with the Adversary System in a Postmodern, Multicultural World." *William and Mary Law Review* 38 (1996): 5–44.

Miller, Janine. "The Canadian Legal Information Institute—A Model for Success." *Legal Information Management* 8, no. 4 (2008): 280–82.

Mullan, David. "The Supreme Court of Canada and Tribunals—Deference to the Administrative Process: A Recent Phenomenon or a Return to Basics?" *Canadian Bar Review* 80 (2001): 399–432.

Orwell, George. "Politics and the English Language." https://www.mtholyoke.edu/acad/intrel/orwell46.htm.

Pencak, William J., Ralph Lindgren, Roberta Kevelson, and Charles N. Yood eds. *"The Law" vs. "The People:" Twelfth Round Table on Law and Semiotics*. New York: Peter Lang, 2000.

Petretti, Vito. "Matthew Bender & Co. v. West Publishing Co.: The End of West's Legal Publishing Empire?" *Villanova Law Review* 43 (1998): 873–922.

Public Legal Education Network and Independent Academic Research Studies. "Measuring Young People's Legal Capability." http://www.lawforlife.org.uk/wp-content/uploads/2013/05/measuring-young-peoples-legal-capability-2009-117.pdf.

Rootman, Irving, and Deborah Gordon-El-Bihbety. *A Vision for a Health Literate Canada: Report of the Expert Panel on Health Literacy*. Ottawa: Canadian Public Health Association, 2008.

Scalia, Antonin, and Bryan A. Garner. *Making Your Case: The Art of Persuading Judges*. Saint Paul, MN.: Thomson-West, 2008.

Scassa, Teresa. "The Best Things in Law are Free?: Towards Quality Free Public Access to Primary Legal Materials in Canada." *Dalhousie Law Journal* 23, no. 2 (2000): 301–36.

Schauer, Frederick F. "Precedent." *Stanford Law Review* 39, no. 3 (1987): 571–605.

———. *Thinking Like a Lawyer: A New Introduction to Legal Reasoning.* Cambridge, MA: Harvard University Press, 2009.

Scriven, Michael. "Methods of Reasoning and Justification in Social Science and Law." *Journal of Legal Education* 23, no. 1 (1971): 189–99.

Silbey, Susan S. "After Legal Consciousness." *Annual Review of Law and Social Science* 1 (2005): 323–68.

Smith, Robert Barr. *The Literate Lawyer: Legal Writing and Oral Advocacy.* 4th Rev. ed. Lake Mary, FL.: Vandeplas, 2009.

Soifer, Aviam. "Beyond Mirrors: Lawrence Friedman's Moving Pictures." *Law & Society Review* 21 (1998): 995–1016.

Staudt, Ronald W., and Paula L. Hannaford. "Access to Justice for the Self-Represented Litigant: An Interdisciplinary Investigation by Designers and Lawyers." *Syracuse Law Review* 52 (2002): 1017–47.

Stem Legal Web Enterprises Inc. Canadian Law Blogs List. *Lawblogs.ca.* (weblog). http://www.lawblogs.ca/.

Stratman, James F. "The Emergence of Legal Composition as a Field of Inquiry: Evaluating the Prospects." *Review of Educational Research* 60, no. 2 (1990): 153–235.

Sullivan, Ruth. "The Promise of Plain Language Drafting." *McGill Law Journal* 47 (2001): 97–128.

Tapp, June Louin, and Felice J. Levine. "Legal Socialization: Strategies for an Ethical Legality." *Stanford Law Review* 27, no. 1 (1974): 1–72.

Ten Brink, Charles J. "A Jurisprudential Approach to Teaching Legal Research." *New England Law Review* 39 (2005): 307–16.

Thibaut, John, and Laurens Walker. "A Theory of Procedure." *California Law Review* 66, no. 3 (1978): 541–66.

Tiersma, Peter M. *Legal Language.* Chicago: University of Chicago Press, 1999.

Tyler, Tom R. "What is Procedural Justice? Criteria Used by Citizens to Assess the Fairness of Legal Procedures." *Law & Society Review* 22, no. 1 (1988): 103–36.

———. "Citizen Discontent with Legal Procedures: A Social Science Perspective on Civil Procedure Reform." *American Journal of Comparative Law* 45, no. 4 (1997): 871–904.

Verkuil, Paul R. "A Study of Informal Adjudication Procedures." *University of Chicago Law Review* 43, no. 4 (1976): 739–96.

——. "The Emerging Concept of Administrative Procedure." *Columbia Law Review* 78, no. 2 (1978): 258–329.

Waluchow, Wil. "Indeterminacy." *Canadian Journal of Law & Jurisprudence* 9 (1996): 397–409.

White, James Boyd. "The Invisible Discourse of the Law: Reflections on Legal Literacy and General Education." *University of Colorado Law Review* 54 (1983): 143–59.

White, Lucie E. "Subordination, Rhetorical Survival Skills, and Sunday Shoes: Notes on the Hearing of Mrs. G." *Buffalo Law Review* 38, no. 1 (1990): 1–58.

WorldLII. "Declaration on Free Access to Law." http://www.worldlii.org/worldlii/declaration/.